Discourses on African Affairs

Discourses on African Affairs

Directions and Destinies for the 21st Century

Okello Oculi

Africa World Press, Inc.

P.O. Box 1892
Trenton, NJ 08607

P.O. Box 48
Asmara, ERITREA

Africa World Press, Inc.

P.O. Box 1892
Trenton, NJ 08607

P.O. Box 48
Asmara, ERITREA

Copyright © 2000 Okello Oculi

First printing 2000

Book Design: Wanjiku Ngugi
Cover Design: Jonathan Gullery

Library of Congress Cataloging-in-Publication Data

Oculi, Okello, 1942-
    Discourses on African affairs : directions and destinies for the 21st century / by Okello Oculi.
        p. cm.
    Includes bibliographical references and index.
    ISBN 0-86543-556-1 (HB) . --ISBN 0-86543-557-X (PB)
        1. Africa--Politics and government--1960- 2. Africa--Economic conditions--1960- I. Title.
DT30.5.O28 1997
960.3'2--dc21   97-47060
                                                 CIP

CONTENTS

Okello Oculi:
The Artist in the Scientist

It is only appropriate that one of the essays in this collection of striking and intriguing titles should be called "The African Novelist as a Spy," a variation on the famous Achebe essay on the Novelist as a Teacher, because Okello Oculi first burst on to East Africa's intellectual scene as a poet and novelist. Even then, his novel, *Prostitute*, marked him out as a social spy. Here was one of Africa's young intellectuals of the sixties who, from the exclusive Makerere College, an institution manufacturing the new postcolonial elite, was looking at the post-independence era from the standpoint of the socially marginalized. His poetry and prose were marked with satiric wit and social insights, two of the most outstanding features of *Discourses on African Affairs* as it is of his earlier book, *Food and the African Revolution*. The discourses range over a variety of subjects and they take the entire Africa as their province. But they are united by some basic concerns.

Of prime interest is Oculi's identification with the dispossessed. So, whether he is looking at or citing events in Somalia, Zaire, Nigeria, Kenya, Uganda, Egypt, he is driven by the same sympathies. He is, of course, horrified at the machinations of imperialism in its colonial and neo-colonial forms. In *Food and the African Revolution*, he had talked a great deal about the exploitation of African labor as the basis of the imperialist manufacture of subsequent famines in Africa. He was not only talking about the role of African labor in the construction of the Americas and post-Renaissance Europe, but also of the development of colonial capitalism in Africa for the benefit of colonizing Europe: African labor as transportation of goods in the pre-railway era; African labor in the building of the new infrastructures; African labor in the colonial armies; African labor, that is virtually free labor, in the colonial plantations. All this meant diversion of African labor from production for self-sustenance and self-reliance into production to meet the needs of others.

His concern with Africa's self-reliance, particularly in the area of food, continues in these essays. For him all the images of a famine stricken Africa, an Africa torn by rival ethnicities, horrifying as they are should not cripple Africa through a debilitating sense of shame but should burn us with new angers and new resolves for a resurgent Africa. He warns us that despite the end of the Cold War imperialist intrigues do not really want a resurgent Africa but rather one that is beholden to American dollars, creating, for instance, dollar democracies instead of social institutions rooted in the people. However, it is for the African people themselves to take up the challenge and to dare to imagine a different Africa. Africa must dare to dream big and to imagine a united Africa in a federal structure at the beginning of the twenty-first century.

The gallery of the historical characters that pop up in these pages are many. Quite a number, like Mobutu of Zaire (now Congo), are no longer on the scene. In that sense the essays may sound dated, especially when the sub-title is *Directions and Destinies For the 21st Century*. But such an impression would be misleading. Most of these figures have been important players, for better or for worse, in the Africa of the latter half of the twentieth century, and there can be no meaningful talk of new directions and destinies of Africa without a careful analysis of the gains and losses in the twentieth century. A necessary part of that analysis is the class factor in African politics and its relations to issues of democracy and social justice within the nation state and with imperialism and international class forces. One would like to see more analysis of the class factor behind so much of what goes under ethnic ideologies and consciousness.

Okello Oculi's discourses should spur new debates on these issues of Africa's decolonization. He writes that now is the time for food and political imagination. These essays have a lot of food for thought as he warns African intellectuals against falling into the traps of mercenarism and challenges them to dare to dream again for a united self-reliant Africa in the twenty-first century. Many intellectuals are now employees of foreign NGO's, the secular missionaries of neo-imperialism, and this relationship between African intellectuals and these secular missionaries may very well meet one of the foreign policy needs of capitalist fundamentalism, the driving force behind neo-imperialism, which is to create states which are too weak to interfere with operations of international finance capital but strong enough to hold back the populace should it dare to intervene and call for a different direction in the economic, political and cultural practices of the nation.

These are well-written essays by a political head with an artist's hand and should make good reading for the specialist as well as the general reader.

—Ngugi wa Thiong'o
Erich Maria Remarque Professor of Languages &
Professor of Comparative Literature and Performance Studies,
New York University

1

SOMALIA, RACISM, AND THE AFRICAN DIASPORA

> Violence is basic to African society and its environment.
> It thrives on the black man's docile acceptance of brutal-
> ity and sudden death. It lurks in the beer pot, behind the
> steering wheel, at funerals and initiation ceremonies and
> in the bridal night. It leaves the poor man bleeding in the
> gutter. No one stops to help him; the man is poor, he is
> unknown, and the ordinary citizen has learned that the
> police station is a place better to avoid.[1]

Does the name sound drums in our memories? Denis Hills was
the British captive Idi Amin threatened to kill as a ploy for luring
the British Foreign Secretary, James Callagahn, into Uganda and
having him photographed on his knees in apparent supplication
to "The Conqueror of the British Empire," as Amin titled himself. Denis Hills' Africa (as exemplified by Uganda), is brutal
and perpetually nude. In his Africa, a white woman "making educated conversation" with a member of the African elite, also

sees "a naked savage with a penis a foot long." The white woman in Africa (including Nobel Prize winner Nadine Gordimer) both fears being and longs to be raped by a Black man. This is because she also carries in her "an unconscious desire to stop thinking and let the body take over." This sensual lapse Africa is ready to offer her. Finally, she (and her other white kin) discovers that in Africa *her color is a force*, a "non-violent assertion," which makes her "special" among Africans.

The American writer Paul Theroux (who himself had taught at Makerere University in Uganda) attributes to Denis Hills "the realization that he is white in a Black country, and respected for it."[2]

That realization is often "capitalized" upon by many expatriates. Underlying this attitude is the sense of security he feels in the confirmation of prejudices back home of Europeans being "superior persons"—the "god from across the seas with large brain and fragile body,"stalking Africa.

The prejudices of race are back as the weapon—the ideology—of the post-Cold War era. The Germans in East Germany, whose social security and sense of being important to society and the socialist state have gone, are being fed with xenophobia in exchange for factories, which have been closed and mass unemployment. A woman chemical engineer who now earns a living as a prostitute in Moscow or Prague says on BBC that she hates Africans for the Russian or Czechoslovak education they are getting. In Spain, a Black woman nurse from the Dominican Republic was beaten and stabbed to death by Spanish youths. Germans, Spaniards, and British folk who remember the genocides carried out under Hitler and Franco are out in the streets in their thousands, fighting against this officially-encouraged tide of racism and fascism now sweeping over Europe.

In the midst of all this comes the constant barrage of television picture horror-news from Yugoslavia (especially Bosnia), Peru, Colombia, Afghanistan, Armenia... then South Africa, and Somalia. The peoples involved are always either at the rims of Europe—the African-Europeans—or else indigenous to Asia or Africa proper. The murders of Turks in Germany are merely part of a continuum of racist contempt which leads down through Southern Italy to Somalia and South Africa. Choreographed landings of American Marines into Somalia fused raw savagery, irresponsibility, and unfitness to protect human decency with the Tarzan-Redeemers come to exercise civilizing restraint and commitment to human freedom. White power is taking Africa again to make it safe for history's perpetual juvenile delinquents themselves.

The news of the bravado of American Marines is punctuated by those of the brutalizing use of ethnic wrath incarnated in soldiers drawn exclusively from Mobutu's tribe (in Zaire), Eyadema (in Togo), and Arap Moi (in Kenya) in order to thwart free and fair elections. In the Sudan, born-again Moslem fundamentalists dream of dipping their own religious ecstasies into the source of the Nile in Uganda and Tanzania. Twenty-seven years of civil war must not stop yet. The politics of dictatorship is a zero-sum affair. In Liberia the BBC fans the voice of Charles Taylor as the heroic Dracula of West Africa. He is on first-name terms with BBC broadcasters. Taylor reminds readers of V.S. Naipaul's pitiless depiction of African politicians:

> The order to which the colonial politician succeeds is not
> his order. It is something he is compelled to destroy; de-
> struction comes with his emergence and is a condition of
> his power.[3]

The BBC celebrates Charles Taylor and Jonas Savimbi for their violence without a philosophy in their heads and hearts. The era of Samora Machel, Amilcar Cabral, and Augustinho Neto, which gave Africans determination to die for freedom the same dignity in world history as the sacrifices of the Vietnamese and Chinese under Mao, is to be buried by the BBC and VOA. Only mindless African violence is historical now. The violence of IMF and World Bank structural adjustment programs is not historical to the BBC, Radio France, etc.

The signals are alarming. One such signal was the news from the OECD officials that there would be more unemployment in Europe in 1993. IBM alone would throw out 25,000 more employees in 1993. How would the anger and frustrations of hundreds of millions unemployed in Europe be handled? Would voices of new Empires for Democracy turn the Somalia war drills for "Operation Restore Hope" into a full march across Africa? Would the new distraction be lower class white color as "a force" in the tropics?

For those in Africa who are crafting policies aimed at wooing the African Diaspora, the overlapping pictures of starving Somalia and of Tarzan as a Redeemer in tortured Africa form a terrible nightmare. For centuries African-Brazilians, African-Americans, African-Guatamalans, etc., were fed a steady diet of Africa the anti-progress.

Carol Foster, an undergraduate classmate at Stanford University on America's west coast asked me to imagine the humiliation she felt in her racially mixed class when the teacher told the class to open a particular page. On the page were pictures of representatives of the ancestors of the human race. The European ancestor was dressed in a Roman toga; the Asian ancestor in a Japanese Kimono; the African ancestor was naked. But, she was not giving up yet on her race. Years later her uncle visited Ghana. He came back with stories of a land where all bank officials were Black people; the police, government civil servants, etc. were all Black people! And all spoke impeccable English, better than many poor whites he had seen in England, and, of course, the United States itself. Her uncle gave back to her that pride in her race, which had been so shaken at Stanford, where nobody mentioned that her Black ancestors in Ancient Egypt had invented clothes centuries before Europeans. Such stories are out there by the millions. And overcoming the psychological damage done is a task yet to be accomplished.

The struggle, obviously, must not only continue; now—after Somalia and Liberia and Sudan and South Africa, etc.—it must start afresh and with new strategies, starting with mobilizing African children in schools, colleges, and universities for "save Somalia, save Zaire, save South Africa, save Algeria, save Rwanda," etc. rallies, collections, and aid to the stricken here on the continent. As some nameless social critic put it centuries ago, "physician, heal thyself first!"

Notes

1. Denis Hills, *The White Pumpkin* (New York: Grove Press, 1975) pp 192-193.
2. Paul Theroux, "Tarzan is an Expatriate," *Transition*, Vol 7, No. 32, 1976.
3. Cited in Denis Hills, *op.cit.*

2

DID NIGERIA PRODUCE MOBUTU?

President Mobutu's praise-name (given to him from childhood) takes ones breath away: "*Sese Seko Kuku Ngbendu waza Banga.*" It means "the all-conquering warrior who triumphs over all obstacles." Has he lived up to it, so far? He was born on October 14, 1930, to a father (Alberic Bemany) who was a "cook to a Belgian colonial magistrate" and died in 1938 when young Mobutu was only eight years old. His mother (Mama Yemo), in grief and poverty, left Kinshasa to return to their rural province of Equateur. According to distinguished Mobutu critic Professor Crawford Young,[1] the country's most important medical center (located in the capital Kinshasa) is called Mama Yemo Hospital, presumably in celebration of her special curative gift to the nation.

In 1950, Catholic missionaries expelled Mobutu from school. He was nineteen. They were so alarmed and angry with his wiles that they both threw him out of school and got him conscripted into the colonial army for "a seven-year disciplinary" cleansing.

Unlike other recruits, he was fluent in French and soon not only got Colonel Marliene to be godfather to his first child, but also got himself posted to an officer training school. It was here that he met Zaire's future officers. He was discharged from the army in 1956 when serving in Kinshasa.

While still in the army in Kinshasa, Mobutu had started writing articles for newspapers under another name. Piere Davister, a Belgian editor of a journal in Kinshasha, quickly took note of Mobutu and helped him to become a journalist on another weekly paper, *Actualites Africaines*. This European connection soon took him to Brussels, in 1959, where he got "an apprenticeship in the colonial propaganda agency, Inforcongo." Before leaving for Brussels, Mobutu had, in 1957, struck up a friendship with Patrice Lumumba, who had recently arrived in Kinshasa. This personal and political friendship earned him an appointment (from Lumumba, in early 1960) as "head of the MNC/L office in Brussels." He was now a former soldier (who had been discharged with the rank of Sergeant-Major, the highest rank to which an African could rise in the colonial army), a journalist, and a politician.

The period 1959–1960 was also the peak of the drama of decolonization in Zaire. Many interested parties with foresight and troubled hearts began to look for allies and friends among Zairians (politicians, university students and graduates, soldiers, etc.) who would hold their hands and troubled hearts through an uncertain future. The American Central Intelligence Agency (CIA) was one such ally. They dispatched Lawrence Devlin to Brussels "to develop Zairian contacts." Lawrence Devlin (a man with a richly endowed name) was to reappear in Kinshasa a mere few weeks before Mobutu's second major military coup in 1965.

Mobutu left Brussels for Kinshasa three weeks before Independence in 1960. Barely one month after Independence the Belgians engineered a mutiny by Zairian soldiers. Mobutu was seen openly pleading with troops to return to barracks. Several times they obeyed him. In July, Lumumba named Mobutu Secretary of State for defense, as well as Chief of Staff. Two months later, President Kasavubu dismissed Lumumba from the Prime Ministership. Lumumba rejected the dismissal. Mobutu moved in and staged his first military coup. The politician Mobutu had abandoned his political party boss Lumumba. He installed an interim government made up primarily of university students and graduates. Mobutu, the ex-soldier journalist, had first made his most intensive and intimate contacts with Zairian university students and graduates while doing his journalism training in Brussels. Kamitatu has claimed that Mobutu, the politician-journalist-military chief with a hinted taste for power, subsequently spat on the face of a captured Lumumba before sending his former boss to Shaba (Katanga) to be murdered by Moise Tshombe. With Lumumba's death also went the only politician who the Belgians and the Americans truly feared because he had led the only nation-wide and radical political party (MNC/L).

And this is where Nigeria comes in. Between 1940 and 1960 the British had dreaded two monsters: (1) that of Marcus Garvey's Black pride and self-esteem combined with the call for a nationalist cry of "Africa for Africans"; (2) that of Gamal Abd-el Nasser's overthrow of Farouk as a corrupt British "running dog" in Egypt, combined with a call for Moslems, Arabs, and Africans to overthrow white domination. While Marcus Garvey's explosive ideas had in earlier decades filtered into Lagos through reports from sailors, as well as via his paper, *Negro World*, the British had always felt confident that they could contain the fallout. But when it came back to Nigeria as Nnamdi Azikiwe, with a fire-spitting oratory and *West African* political daily newspaper, it raised panic in colonial whiskers.[2]

The dark whispers of disaster increased the din of their wings when angry young men caught his political fever and started calling themselves "Zikists." It was naked profanity, deifying an impudent "troublemaker" who outrageously fancied himself a fine speaker of the English language. Were the imposter to confine his flair for English to causing ripples in Lagos lagoons, it would be perfectly tolerable, but he was fostering throughout the whole country a nationalist political movement. British genius would drive this nationalist vision into the twin swamps of tribalism and regionalism.

As a share of a piece of Africa, King Leopold had snatched for the Belgians only Zaire, a vast and rich land. In geographical and ethnic complexities it was similar to Nigeria, Britain's headache in the 1940s and 1950s. British wisdom on containing African nationalism in Nigeria was worth borrowing. And the Belgians borrowed it with a vengeance and vileness of which only inhabitants of a small swampy country are capable. Between 1957 and 1960 they created monsoon storms of tribalism: in Kinshasa

the Kongo were fighting the Ngala; in Kananga the Lulua were
wrestling with the Luba; in Mbandaka it was Mongo against the
Ngome; and in Lubumbashi the "authentic Katangans" were slapping Kasaians. These were tribal skirmishes in the major towns.
Every ethnic patch in every village soon became political com-
batants against other "enemies." Those Luba who lived down-
stream on the Zaire River (Bena Tshibanda) became political
enemies of upstream Luba (Bena Mutu Wa Mukuna).

Belgian District Officers and secret service were so successful in cultivating tribal "fears and insecurities" (and often open
violence) that the 1960 national election for independence in Zaire
was contested by over 250 political parties. The last election, in
1965 (after which Mobutu struck), was contested by 233 political parties. Some might say that the Nigerian infection of Zaire's
politics had been so severe and debilitating that Nigeria owes
Zaire substantial reparations. Between 1960 and 1965, elected
politicians in Zaire at national and provincial levels virtually went
berserk with tribalism. "Particular ministries," writes one observer,
"had become ethnic fiefdoms."[3]

Herein lies Mobutu's genius and historic claims on Zairian
nationalism. In changing the name of a wrecked country from
Belgian Congo to Zaire he was expressing a new hope for a nation. In getting his people to drop their Christian names, he was
slapping the face of a Catholic Church, which had expelled the
likes of him from its school system, as well as taken part in incit-
ing destructive tribalism all across the country in immoral collusion with Belgians and international financiers and companies.
He was asking his people to chant: "The country is the heritage
of our ancestors."

Between 1960 and 1965 Zaire had murdered Lumumba (its
charismatic leader who was also respected all across Africa); killed
Dag Hammarskjold (the Swedish United Nations Secretary General) in a mysterious plane crash; fought a war of secession in
which Moise Tshombe had used white mercenaries; and been
occupied by arrogant United Nations troops and officials. After
all that, Moise Tshombe had returned to become the Prime Minister of a country to which he had brought great tragedy and humiliation. "Tshombe," Young tells us, is a Shaba word for cassava. Moise Tshombe's father started his business by walking
long distances selling cassava, and was awarded the name by a
grateful public. With the help of a Belgian, the old man had become

a millionaire before Independence. His son Moise Tshombe obviously learned the lesson of the benefits of making commercial and political deals with Europeans. Mobutu was obviously not willing to admire such a competitor in the same space and time. His coup of 1965 was to deny Tshombe the Prime Ministership with a new mandate. Tshombe was to be kidnapped from Spain in 1969 and deposited in an Algerian prison where he was to die of a "heart attack."

Mobutu may well have heard (far too often, perhaps) Nigerians making claims of manifest destiny to lead Africa. He too wanted a national ideology, which would give his people a new sense of self-respect. Gowon went to the United Nations as Chairman of the OAU and acted pompous, even important. Mobutu quickly followed. The visitor's gallery at the UN was filled with a forest of the most beautiful women Zaire had bestowed upon humanity. And a music band. Its music swept through the usually grim cobwebs of international diplomacy to hail Mobutu's arrival. At appropriate intervals (inherent in their patriotic memories), female beauty at song to African drums saluted The Guide's speech.

From symbolic showmanship the competition went into the deadly field of economies. Zaire would have a grand steel mill (perhaps to outdo Ajaokuta in Nigeria); the Inga Dam would send electricity all across the length of the country to Shaba's copper mines; then a railway line from Shaba across the country with an extension to Kisangani in the northeast. That road to economic greatness would be paved with huge debts from cheering and chuckling European lenders and, of course, Godfathers IMF and World Bank. Finally, in 1972, Gowon pronounced "Nigerianization-Indegenization of the economy." Worse still for Mobutu, just across the Ruwenzori Mountains Field Marshall Idi Amin had captured the imagination of hungry Black peoples worldwide with his Asian Exodus. Amin captured Asian wealth with nothing but his volcanic mouth as currency. In 1974 "Zairianization" and "Radicalization" also struck in Mobutu's land. Perhaps beating Gowon, for once, Mobutu in 1972 sent a hint to the National Conference of the only—and ruling—political party in the country (MPR) that he wanted to be made (by popular acclamation) President for Life. He did not get it, but he did remain in power while his competitor Gowon left the stage.

Critics of President Mobutu have gotten angrier with time, perhaps even hysterical. If Mobutu keeps a Senegalese diviner he is harangued. When President Reagan patronizes an astrologer it is no threat to democracy. If under President Reagan sharp characters on Wall Street, in defense industries, in housing, run away with billions of American taxpayers' dollars, it is not a threat to democracy. If Mobutu acquires shares in ITT-Bell, Fiat, Gulf, Renault, Peugeot, Volkswagen, and Unilever subsidiaries in Zaire, as well as uses Zairianization to acquire 14 plantations which by 1977 were employing 25,000 laborers (including 140 Europeans), they scream that in Zaire "corruption itself became the system." If by 1978, the wages Zairians earned were ten percent of wages in 1960; if teachers teach for over a year before their salaries arrive; if soldiers in rural areas set up roadblocks to collect ransom from market women or "seize" goods at market places without payment," there is consensus that Mobutu's regime has brought economic ruin to the many. But there is silence over the debt repayments the IMF and European lenders collect faithfully despite their impact on the country. Are these debt repayments any less contemptible and destructive than the fact that by 1980 the scale of embezzlement and stealing of public funds by all government officials in Zaire was over "60 percent of the national budget?"[4]

Should Mobutu be condemned? Yes, but not totally and not without caution. The "pro-democracy" wind is now blowing against him even though the same "windpipe" intervened militarily on his side in 1960, 1964, 1977, 1978. There is no reason to believe that this time the pro-democracies are on the side of the best interests of Zaire. And yet the issue is not that of "pro-democracy" manipulators pursuing their interests. They have every right to. The issue for us is with *the silence of the African politicians all over the continent.* Have they not been studying Zaire, Kenya, Mozambique, Angola, Ghana, Nigeria, Tanzania, Algeria, Egypt, Ethiopia, etc.? Do African politicians have heroes and villains, or do they merely wait for Radio Moscow, BBC, VOA, Radio China to tell them what to know about Africa, when to think? If politics is a vocation, does it not call for the effort to research, to know, to hear and see Africa, and then think about her, for her? Does political independence not imply intellectual duties and obligations (in front of world history) by the African politician?

The African peasant, small trader, shoe-repairer, taxi-driver, the unemployed in villages and towns, etc. have been aware of their duties and obligations. It is to survive and sustain hope in their children. The African politician must seize history and get us out of the following predicament, poignantly perceived by a Zairian intellectual as follows:

> Africa moves between religiosity and cheating, between praying and stealing—praying at night and stealing during the day. Praying Africa awaits the miracle and urges it as a solution to illness, poverty and wretchedness. That is the Africa of the night, of Saturdays and Sundays. The Africa of the week and the day manages to get along, the corrupters and the corrupted dying between two worlds in search of survival.[5]

Whether or not Nigeria begot President Mobutu (and his other African types) deserves intellectual investment from Nigeria's politicians, journalists, and intellectuals, apart from those in Foreign Affairs and the Presidency.

Notes

1. Crawford Young & Thomas Turner, *The Rise and Decline of the Zairean State*, (The University of Wisconsin Press, 1985), provide considerable incriminating data against President Mobutu and his regime. The bulk of the data here is from their works.
2. Alkassum Abba in a personal communication urged on me the thesis that Nnamdi Azikiwe was perceived by British colonial officials as a political threat who was courtable with monthly rituals of Zik, playing a game of tennis and laters sipping tea with the Colonial Governor of Nigeria.
3. Michael G. Schatzberg, *Politics and Class in Zaire: Bureaucracy, Business, and Beer in Lisala.* (New York: Africana Publishing, 1980).
4. Ibid.
5. Illunga Kabongo cited in Bayat.

3

YANKEES AGAINST BRITS
IN KENYAN POLITICS

Did the Americans lose, yet again, in their bid to control Kenyan politics? The Mau Mau war against European settlers in Kenya lost militarily against overwhelming British bombings and hauling of thousands of the civilian population into concentration camps. The guerilla movement was denied "the water" in which to do its political swimming. But it won the *political* war by dooming the political future of the European settlers in Kenya. Both the British government and the leading groups among the European settlers, however, quickly scrambled for new ways of cutting their losses. The British threatened Jomo Kenyatta (then in prison) with rumors of plots to assassinate him in prison, as well as to deny him the leadership of post-colonial Kenya. Outside the prison walls they urged Oginga Odinga to abandon Kenyatta. His refusal to tango with the British meant that two majority ethnic groups (the Gikuyu and the Luo), would stay solidly behind the dreaded Jomo Kenyatta. Above all, it promised the coming of a politics of radical attack on European settlers' control of the best agricultural land in Kenya when colonial rule was over. The intensified rumors of assassination plots on Kenyatta appears to have gotten results. He promised to abandon the radical program of the Mau Mau war.

Sir Michael Blundel and other European settler leaders also decided to put up a fight against a fatal Kenyatta-Oginga Odinga victory. They invented Daniel Arap Moi (a primary school teacher from the Rift Valley), and Ronald Ngala from the shores of the Indian Ocean. If the Gikuyu-Luo alliance would not crumble, then they would create a crack in the nationalist movement by fanning fears of the "majority tribes" dominating the "minority tribes" forever after the British had left. The Moi-Ngala alliance became a party known as the Kenya African Democratic Union (KADU), pitched against the Kenyatta-Oginga's Kenya African National Union (KANU).

KADU preached confederation, while KANU stood for National Unity under one central administration. Twenty-eight years later Moi had become the national unitarist and Oginga the democrat. How did it all happen?

The British plot won the day in 1964. Kenyatta's KANU won, but he immediately called for a Kenya of Africans "suffering without bitterness." The European settlers should have no fears; their interests were safe. But to make assurance doubly sure, Oginga Odinga lost his vice-presidency. It was probably at this point that the Americans entered the fracas. The tempo of Kenyan politics had the smell of the Western Cowboy good guys running the bad guys out of town. The then American Ambassador, Atwood, hated Oginga Odinga. He saw him as a communist, the tool of the Russians and the Chinese. If he got rid of him, he would position their own man (the handsome, charismatic and very articulate Tom Mboya), for succeeding the now old Kenyatta. Tom Mboya was a Luo like Oginga, and Oginga had squashed his muted ambition to abandon Kenyatta in jail and grab the leadership of KANU.

Two years after Independence Mboya mangled constitutional provisions and ran Oginga out of the vice-presidency *and* out of the party. The callousness of the political drama left deep wounds. Oginga Odinga and Bildad Kaggia formed their own party, the Kenya Peoples Union (KPU). Those members of parliament who left KANU with them had their seats in Parliament declared vacant.

In any event, KPU was soon banned and thereafter Kenya became a one-party state by legislation. Arap Moi had quietly moved into the post of minister of police and prisons. In his own good time he would occupy the vice-presidency, which had once been Oginga's. The Americans suffered their first major defeat in the drama of Kenyan politics when their star player Tom Mboya was gunned down in broad daylight on a busy street in Nairobi. After the tears had dried, Kenyatta and Moi (the wards of Britain and the European Settlers) were together safely ensconced. The police and the prisons assumed new political hatchet duties.

Oginga Odinga was an obstacle to one of Kenyatta's cherished dreams: the creation of a monarchy and an aristocracy in Kenya. He had told the *London Times Sunday Magazine* in 1968 that as a student in London he had come to admire the stability which the monarchy gave British society. He would create one in Kenya. He appears to have gone about achieving this objective in two ways: making members of his Kiambu clan wealthy (as the core of the monarchy), and making all top civil servants and members of parliament rich by giving them money with which to buy land from departing European farmers, as well as shares in parastatals (as the aristocratic classes-to-be). For this to succeed he had to kill the party (KANU) which Oginga Odinga had associated in popular aspirations with giving back land to the landless masses of Kenya after Uhuru (Independence). He allowed party branches at the grassroots level to decay, and held no party conference at any level. There must be no forum for the masses to censure his government ministers and officials. The President's Men (ministers, police officers, and provincial commissioners) became answerable to Kenyatta himself and not to parliament. When parliamentarians threatened to become rude, its most dangerous members suddenly became fond of dying in car accidents. Pio Gama Pinto was allowed the rare privilege of being shot in front of his own house.

To ward off total mass disenchantment with politics and government, Kenyatta (popularly addressed as *Mzee*, "our elder") allowed competitive electoral politics within the one-party sack of candidates he took to the people. It became the tradition in successive elections for a large number of his unprotected ministers to lose elections. People felt good every five years, but the politics of building a clan-based monarchy and a national aristocracy remained on track. *Mzee* Kenyatta was also a brilliant anthropologist.

He knew that the African electorate wanted "to eat from their man in power." Left on their own, however, his new aristocrats would not remember to take the food to their voters in the villages. So he invented the *Harambee* practice by which each man-of-power (ministers and members of parliament) would go to villages and contribute funds for building schools, clinics, etc. This was the service ventilation for containing the frustrations and anger of the masses now that their party structures were moribund. The catch in *Harambee* politics was that you had to have the money to donate; and Kenyatta was the cashier. Be rude to *Mzee* and you lose the next election. Lose an election and you lose your window into the politics of building an aristocracy.

However, the Gikuyu (Kenyatta's ethnic group) were perceived as having benefited the most. Arap Moi was a good student under Kenyatta. He too ran pretenders to Kenyatta's throne "out of town" and out of power (especially former Attorney General Charles Njonjo and Kenyatta's nephew Njoroge Mungai.) Then he began to openly build his own Kalenjin ethnic monarchy. With the service windows from state power increasingly closed to them, the Kenyatta aristocrats cried foul and became increasingly hysterical. Whereas Charles Njonjo had made it a treasonable offense to criticize *Mzee* Kenyatta (and even to speculate about his age), Moi lacked that mystique and protective cocoon. His relationships with his cronies lacked political immunity. Some of his ethnic beneficiaries, notably Oloitiptip, even took the wicked liberty of becoming physically very fat, automatically triggering other people's appetites each time they saw him.

Moi's alleged interest in the death of his Foreign Minister Ouko (who was apparently being groomed by the Americans as Moi's successor) was openly denounced by his political opponents, many of whom did not dare to publicly link Kenyatta with Tom Mboya's murder. The death of Robert Ouko also brought out the crudest combative instincts in the American ambassador. Taking his cue from President George Bush's roller-coaster mauling of Panama's President Noriega, the envoy openly instructed President Moi to control his "political thugs" and then garlanded him with ethnic election violence and murders. It looked as if Moi would lose the elections.

The appearance, however, hid Moi's skillful use of the Kenyatta-based politics of creating ethnic aristocracies for rebuilding his confederate constituency of the 1954-1966 era into a national centralizing force. While Oginga Odinga was allowing himself the indignity of adopting the American-tainted label of "Forum for the Restoration of Democracy" (FORD), Moi was reviving Michael Blundel's drumbeats of the Gikuyu-Luo majority ethnic groups, plotting to exclude all the ethnic minorities from "also eating power." When the British in 1991/92 sent Kenneth Matiba back to Kenya from London (and orchestrated a motorcade welcome for him from the airport to Nairobi) as the Gikuyu candidate against Oginga Odinga for the leadership of FORD, they succeeded precisely where they had failed in pre-independence Kenyan politics. The Gikuyu-Luo alliance was shattered. With that success they torpedoed the ramshackle FORD truck, which the Americans had put on the bumpy road of Kenyan politics.

The real question now is about the future of this "FORD-Truck Democracy," which the Americans have brought back into Kenyan politics. It has introduced into Kenya bitter and bloody interethnic politics. Kenyatta had overcome confederation politics, choking it with his drive to create a national aristocracy. Kenyan politics of an earlier period, had known Black people (Mau Mau) shooting white people (and their hierling Black soldiers) rather than ethnic group killing ethnic group or Islam being used as a political rallying cry on the Kenyan coast.

In the 1992–1997 period, the opposition parties in parliament must deliver services to their electors. Moi cannot be expected to do this on their behalf. If they cannot deliver services, then their chances of winning votes again in 1998 are slim. People do not eat abuses and accusations against Moi. Will the electorate trek back with their begging bowls to KANU? Or should we expect the Americans to invent a Kenya Politics Investment Fund (KPIF) for ensuring loans to opposition politicians for financing development projects in their individual constituencies? Will the Cold War era be replaced by American-funded "Dollar Politics for Democracy" all over Africa? One certainly hopes not, for puppet civilian regimes and political leaders will never be the material needed to build a truly African democratic politics. Kenyan politicians should now be encouraged to have a dialogue, which will enable their politics to pull back from the twin horrors of a politics of perpetual ethnic violence, and puppet dollar politicking.

Notes

1. Atieno Odhiambo, "Tom Mboya 1930-1969:Trade Unionist, Nationalist, Pan Africanist, and Government Minister in Kenya 1953-1969," in Harvey Glickman (ed). *Political Leaders in Contemporary Africa South of the Sahara: A Biographical Dictionary* (Greenwood Press, 1992). Odhiambo credits Mboya with having "the open society" as his vision: "What he did was to sanctify competitive politics as a feature of public life in Kenya." The facts say the opposite. His driving Oginga Odinga and his supporters out of KANU, the ruling party, as well as out of Parliament as soon as they formed the KPU opposition party hardly suggest political openness.

4

CAN THE BOER BE A PAN-AFRICANIST?

On February 3, 1909, Jan Smuts, that rare combination of a brilliant military commander and politician, uttered these words:

> In the creative Spirit of History the blunders of men are
> often more valuable than their profoundest wisdom....From
> the blood and tears of nations, which human passions have
> caused she proceeds calmly and dispassionately to build
> up new nations and to lead them along new undiscovered
> paths of progress. And when the darkness of the night has
> passed at last and the light of a new national conscious-
> ness dawns, the scales fall from men's eyes, they perceive
> that they have been led, that they have been borne forward
> in the darkness by deeper forces than they ever apprehended
> to a larger goal that they ever conceived, and they stand
> silent in the presence of that greatest mystery in the world,
> the birth of the soul of a new nation.[1] (Hancock 1962:265)

Watching the Nigerian national team, the Green Eagles, coached by a white Dutchman, play against a South African national team, which was predominantly Black and coached by a Black man from Peru, in the Transvaal, the heartland of Boer nationalism, I wondered if Smuts might have foreseen this cauldron of paradoxes, over eighty years ago. Smuts was so brilliant that he set a record in the history of passing law degree examinations at Cambridge University in Britain. But, he was not brilliant enough to forge a united *African-Boer* army to fight British imperialism in the 1899-1902 Anglo-Boer War. It was instead the British who supplied arms to the Africans to help them defeat the Boers. After the war, Smuts approved British treachery in *disarming* their African allies, but not their Boer adversaries. Nor did his brilliance stop him from excluding Africans from voting or being voted for in South African politics. Did Smuts carry within him an eternal tribal Boer hatred for the African?

An old Boer tribal slogan says: "Then shall it be, from Simonsberg to the Zambesi, Africa for the Afrikanders." It is at once territorial in ambition and domineering in its tribal assertiveness. Some have said that territorial expansionism was first stamped into the souls of bewildered Boer settlers who came ashore at the Cape of Good Hope in 1652. Their leader, Jan Riebeck, is reported to have planted a row of trees to separate the location his small tribal band had settled on, from the indigenous Shoeshor, thus baptizing the land with the viciously selfish core of apartheid. Like all migrant tribes, they immediately combined the lure of begging with the brutal boldness of armed robbery to acquire cattle, sheep, and goats. *And land.* As all cattle rearers know, the milk of a cow is the dew of religion. With stomachs full with milk from looted Zulu cows, the Boer soon saw a religious vision of God anointing his race as the carriers of His Divine Will to rob, kill, and torment Africans, in the name of building a civilization.

But, the Boer today protests at any hint of doubting his being native to Africa. The official propaganda asserts that among the thousands of tribes on the African continent, it is only the Boer's who have adopted the name of the whole continent as their official name—the Afrikaans. All other tribes simply suffer from territorial trachoma. Moreover, they insist that in two world wars they have shed Boer blood in the service of a greater "*African nation*" below the Zambezi. In the 1914-1917 World War, both

Smuts and his Prime Minister Botha commanded South African troops, which ended German rule in today's Namibia. If the Germans were out, South-West Africa would become part of South Africa, so Smuts and Botha dreamt. By March 1916, Smuts was commanding a British army of 45,000 (including 20,000 South Africans) in German East Africa (now Tanzania). The secret of South African military enthusiasm in that arena is mirrored in a letter to Smuts. "If that country were conquered by us," the letter said, "we could probably effect an exchange with Mozambique and so consolidate our territories South of the Zambezi and Kunene." Was it the wrath of Smuts' spirit and all the spirits of the Boer soldiers who fought (and many died) in German East Africa that shot down the aircraft, which was carrying President Samora Machel of Mozambique over eight decades later? And from 1976 to 1994 heartlessly ruined Mozambique? Does the territorial expansionism of the Boer in its loving the lands of a continent also forever negate in Boer souls the humanity of the African owners of these lands? Is the God of the Boer forever a divine grave digger for the African?

But Smuts would protest at such a conclusion. It is too deadended. It does not allow for the optimism of History. History, he would say, climbs on that ladder, which "the blood and tears of nations, which human passions" are constantly erecting. But, where are the hands of hope? Well, Smuts fought with his Boer tribe against British occupation. They were defeated , but out of that defeat his people elected him and his boss, Botha, to lead the only other federal Union on the African continent, which together with the Nigerian federation, have survived the end of British rule. Out of the bitterness of inter-tribal Boer against English-speakers, hatred and bloodshed and both Boer and English together against the Africans, Coloreds, and Indians, the Union of South Africa has continued to survive and grow. Surely, this is territorialism locking hands with a nation larger than the Boer's fears.

The Boer, as a farmer, came to hate the British for coming to loot gold and diamonds from his part of Africa. He shed blood to chase them away. When he lost the war he fought with tribal solidarity and wrath to wrest as big a chunk of that wealth from the hideous and greedy British capitalists for his own people in Africa. To sharpen the ethnic horns of their drive they abandoned Dutch as their official and national language in favor of Afrikaans—

a pidgin vernacular. As part of his contribution to this ethnic nationalism (for a place in the sun of world politics), Smuts is credited with giving birth to the idea of a British Commonwealth of nations in opposition to plans for establishing a post-war British Imperial Federation. The idea of Commonwealth would recognize the sovereign independence and equality of the South African "Boer" nation with those of Canada, Australia, Britain, India, new Zealand. Surely, here was economic nationalism, nationalism of mother tongue, and the nationalism of the Boer "keeping his eyes on the prize" of national independence. And for we other colonized Africans too, later.

But, all this is still within the territory of a barren land of Boer hatred for other races and "narrow-minded exclusiveness." Is Pan-Africanism not more than this mere ethnic, economic, linguistic, and political territorialisms; as well as the perception of brutal ethnic selfishness as the motor of civilization? South African construction companies, retail companies dealing in consumer goods, sugar-producing companies, car and truck manufacturers, mineral prospectors, etc., may now want an *African Union Government* as the big policeman to protect their investments in the Africa of the twenty-first century. Drinking palmwine and rushing down hot-peppered *eshewu*, and crocodile-eye pepper-soup as they dip their toes into the Atlantic Ocean off the Senegalese coast, they will want African Union Government policemen and magistrates to protect their moneyed belches into the sunset. But does money-territorialism wipe away race hatred from the bowels of a Boer capitalist or *hoggenheimer* (to use the Afrikaans lingua)?

The Young Mahatma Gandhi was pushed from a railway station platform and into a gutter by a Boer racist. He was also thrown off a moving train because he was sitting by a cabin reserved for whites only. Out of these experiences, and those of his fellow Indians, the young brilliant lawyer invented *satyagraha* or non-violence. And he first tested its power in racist South Africa. It won its first major battle, however, by making the British look like the barbarians they were in faraway colonial India. Dr. Martin Luther King, Jr., in the 1960s, was to use it successfully in fighting for the freedom of African-Americans in the faraway United States. Its failure in South Africa was to give moral justification to Nelson Mandela's escalation to armed struggle.

But surely we are entitled to demand a *satyagraha* against Boer racial hatred and "narrow-minded exclusiveness" from within the Afrikaaner community itself. Surely, only thus can we ever stop worrying that the Afrikaaner has perhaps forever killed sleep in Africa. That the Nigerian national team even had a chance to compete in the 1994 World Cup was in itself a victory of that nation's desperate prayer over the exclusionary efforts of South Africa's Bafana Bafana. On that day, we were all *truly* "in the presence of that greatest mystery in the world, the birth of the soul of a New [Pan-African] nation."

Notes

1. A sympathetic treatment of Jan Smuts is in W.K. Hancock, *Smuts: The Sanguine Years 1870-1919* (London: Cambridge University Press, 1962). On May 15, 1917, Smuts articulated his notion of a British Commonwealth, to the Joint Houses of Parliament, thus:

   "I think that we are inclined to make mistakes about this group of nations to which we belong because too often we think about it as one state. We are not a State. The British Empire is much more than a State. I think the very expression 'Empire' is misleading, because it makes people think that we are one community, to which the term Empire can appropriately be applied. Germany is an Empire. Rome was an Empire. India is an Empire. But, we are a system of nations. We are not a State, but a community of States and nations. We are a system of States and not a stationary but a dynamic and evolving system, always going forward to new destinies.... Let us take the name Commonwealth. All the empires we have known in the past and that exist today are founded on the idea of assimilation, of trying to force human material into one mold. Your whole idea and basis is entirely different. You do not want to standardize the nations of the British Empire; you want to develop them to fuller, greater nationality...."(431)

5

WILL BILL CLINTON AND SOUTH AFRICA PAY REPARATIONS TO ANGOLA?

With a letter from Maseru, Basutoland (now Lesoto), dated July 20, 1965, the Pan-African Congress (PAC) dismissed its ambassador to Algeria, effective from June 30, 1965. He was accused of being antagonistic to Communist China, which the PAC saw as a natural ally against the Soviet Union, which was supporting its rival, the African National Congress (ANC). The ambassador in question, Patrick Duncan, a white South African in an avowedly *Black Africanist* organization, had just before this humiliating dismissal also had his South African citizenship withdrawn by South African Minister of Justice Verwoerd for being hostile to apartheid. He had escaped from South Africa to Basutoland after the government had banned him from travelling outside of Cape Town. As Duncan was leaving Basutoland for a trip abroad, the British colonial authorities there announced that now he was also prohibited from returning to Basutoland, Bechuanaland, and

Swaziland. Before his dismissal from his ambassadorial post, he had in 1963, travelled to the United States and had both raised a lot of money for the PAC and gotten a personal audience with Attorney General Robert Kennedy (brother to President Kennedy). Kennedy had shown keen interest in his plans to establish military bases in Basustoland and Bechuanaland (Botswana) for guerrilla warfare by the PAC against South Africa's apartheid regime. All this, however, went down in flames when President Kennedy was assassinated. Moreover, the ANC was accusing him of being a CIA agent. With all that drama behind his immediate past, Patrick Duncan said this in a book he decided to write while still in Algeria:

> Only human babies howl. Why? Why is the entry into human society so painful, so much a matter of despair? Could it be a painful impact with the accumulation of a million years of evil?[1]

He was now a bitter man; and yet that was a question the Angolans in the Movement for the Popular Liberation of Angola (MPLA) were probably at the time also putting Duncan to the racist regime in South Africa, and to the American and Portuguese governments. Duncan, for his part, had been in Angola in 1961 and shown great friendship and admiration for Holden Roberto, but condemned the MPLA for being communist. He was silent over Holden Roberto's links with the American CIA. He reported, in his magazine *Contact*, that South Africa had army camps inside Angola "to try to insulate the Southern Ovambo (people) from the northern" (Ovambo)—the latter being the main supporters of SWAPO inside South-West Africa, now Namibia. But what of South Africa already fighting on the side of the colonial Portuguese army so that Angola would remain a perpetual labor camp from which the Portuguese annually sold Black people to go and do slave-labor in the mines and farms of white land owners in South Africa?

Before 1961 (the year the MPLA took up its armed struggle in Angola), South African mining companies and white farmers had collaborated in a scheme for deporting hundreds of thousands of able-bodied Angolans from their country for contract labor in South Africa. While they built South Africa with their labor, their own country and families continued to decay. From 1961 to today, South Africa has been fighting militarily against the MPLA in Angola. Today, she is still fighting, with "white mercenaries" (according to the MPLA government), on the side of Savimbi's UNITA. On the 22nd of January 1993, UNITA bombed the water-works that supplies water to the over three million people in the capital-city, Luanda. They obviously wished to kill the civilian population with epidemic diseases (like cholera and dysentery), which are related to shortages of water and increasing lack of good hygiene, thus destroying infrastructures while using biological warfare against the civilian population in the name of democracy. And this after UNITA had lost an election urged on the MPLA government by the West (friends of apartheid South Africa). The election was declared by United Nations observers to have been "free and fair." The case for computing South Africa's war reparations (both as a collaborator with colonial Portugal in the inhuman sale and exploitation of Angolans as compelled slave labor and as a perpetrator of sustained military destruction of lives and property inside Angola) is clear. And the United Nations should enforce it.

The Americans have peculiar charges to answer. First, is their persistent betrayal of president Woodrow Wilson's 1917 pledge to defend the self-determination of oppressed people everywhere. Everywhere, including Angola. From 1917 to 1961, apart from sending into colonial Angola a handful of Christian missionaries (who started schools for Africans), the Americans would not apply Wilson's call to Angola.

Secondly, during the early Cold War era, America engaged in willful strategic neglect and amnesia. Angola stands across the face of the Atlantic Ocean from the Americans. She also stands on the route around Arab and Persian oilwells. Where enlightened self-interest might have urged a policy of pre-empting nationalist revolution by promoting freedom and development in Angola, racism at home and abroad apparently fertilized sleep and callous collaboration with Portugal. When the MPLA leaders in disgust and disillusionment, however, turned to the Soviet Union for support, the NATO powers (with United States leadership) promptly gave bombers and tanks to Portugal for the "defense of a vital strategic sea-route." The carnage that followed against a defenseless rural African people, has been enormously disgraceful to all preachers of "Western democracy."

And thirdly, the Americans created, and then fuelled, first Holden Roberto (because he is Mobutu's brother-in-law), and later Jonas Savimbi. Savimbi (like Shevernadze in former Soviet Georgia), is still being supported by the West because he lost elections to a "communist." A correspondent of the *Daily Telegraph* said recently on Radio South Africa, that sometime in 1988, Savimbi burnt alive wives of those UNITA officials who he perceived as his rivals for leadership, as well as summarily executed those he could catch. If he can do these atrocious things to UNITA followers, those in MPLA must get genocide. Is the American Government not guilty here (by virtue of having hoisted and sustained Savimbi into world history), of these crimes too? Is the international community not thus entitled to call for reparations to be paid by the United States to the tortured peoples of Angola for such war crimes?

Finally, by the example of its faulty democracy at home, the United States did spread abroad the virus of apartheid. The anthropologist Peter Matthiessen, in his book *In The Spirit of Crazy Horse*[2] (1992 edition), has produced devastating evidence about the utterly cruel and "genocidal way" white America has for over two hundred years treated the Red Indians (now Native Americans).The American army, the judiciary , the Federal Bureau of Investigation (FBI), local State police, white farmers, etc. have separately and collectively killed, robbed, and harassed the Indians. Companies that have mined uranium, coal, and natural gas have had Indians driven away from their lands either into urban ghettos, or onto barren lands. "It would," he writes, "be difficult to find (today) a family without an alcoholic or a member in jail, a recent suicide or car wreck victim, a woman sterilized by the Indian Health Service without her consent, or a child removed to a government boarding school or foster home against the family's will." Jan Smuts (a Boer guerilla war hero and South African Prime Minister) often made reference to United States laws and treatment of non-white racial groups. Others did too as Boer nationalism increased its cruel plunge into apartheid. Patrick Duncan, in 1965, saw a "World-Wide freemasonry of those with white skins" engaged in a grand conspiracy "to preserve in European and white hands a quasi-monopoly of power, wealth and status." If the United States is anxious to claim global reward for promoting "democracy," should the international community also demand of that nation criminal historical responsibility (as manifested by payment of reparations) to immediate and remoter victims of apartheid?

Patrick Duncan was a brilliant Oxford graduate, and son of the first indigenous governor-general of South Africa. He knew about European power, including its global imperial variant. Certainly, recent history seems to prove his case. Saddam Hussein invaded Kuwait and Operation Desert Storm was urgently born by the United Nations of the West and it drowned Iraq in its own blood and debris. South Africa invaded Angola. Operation BBC, VOA, Radio France International, etc., merely fanned the sweating faces of her "New Boer Trekker" soldiers. Saddam Hussein bought a very big and very long pipe. The sun glare from it gave Western spooks a foreboding hint. Their reports home evoked "visions" of Saddam's nuclear bombs not only wiping out Israel and the eastern half of the United States, but also stamping pictures of Saddam's terrible moustache on European and American national currency notes. The United Nations urgently crafted a "Charter For The Return of Iraq To Blissful Scientific Illiteracy."

UN experts are now engaged in demolition carnivals all over that cheeky country. South Africa was caught by Soviet spy satellites exploding a "nuclear device." The United States, Germany, and France were known to have tutored South African scientists with the gift of "enriching uranium." How does the United Nations punish the Boers for such cheek? "RELEASE MANDELA and END APARTHEID! THE ANC AND PAC MUST NOT GO NUCLEAR. But before you do all that, feel free to shoot as many Blacks as you deem a fair measure of your anguish." So thundered the "UN Character for Clipping THE MAD SOULS of The Boers." Nobody is demolishing South Africa's military and scientific arsenals. Not yet.

President Clinton owes a significant part of his 1992 victory to his brilliant grasping of the curve of the "Rainbow Coalition," which Jesse Jackson had aroused in 1984 and 1988. The core of that Rainbow Coalition is the cry for reparations to the oppressed African-American, Indian-American and poor-and-getting-poorer White-American. Those of us who are outside the curve of that Rainbow Coalition do also insist on being part of its shadow, of its silhouette. As the Number-One Super Power today, the United States will be a punching bag for those in the international arena who, (while practising the dictum that "countries are mainly motivated by selfishness in matters of foreign policy") will turn around to drench her with calls for morality in her own actions. Yet, it is also true that the Angolas of this world have, for far too long, been in America's International Rainbow Coalition of exploitation. Sadly, without a Presidency to run for and capture. They too deserve reparations. President Clinton must therefore not be afraid to face that vital change in American foreign policy, which will ensure reparations for the "accumulation of a million years of evil," which the international Rainbow Coalition has known. Today's wrecked Angola is an urgent place to start from. As Maya Angelou urged Clinton, with "poetic majesty" (at his inauguration),

> "Here, on the pulse of this new day
> You may have the grace to look up
> and out
> And into [ANGOLA's] eyes .....
> And say simply
> Very simply
> With hope
> Good morning!"

Notes

1. C.J. Driver, *Patrick Duncan: South African and Pan-African* (London: Heinemann, 1980), p.258.

2. Peter Matthiessen, *In the Spirit of Crazy Horse* (Harvill, 1992).

6

"WHAT TIME IS IT? IT'S NATION TIME!"

Professor Ali Mazrui is probably right in insisting that African geographers are some of our worst enemies. For two reasons: (1) for not inventing an African map of the globe; and (2) for being silent about cartography as a tool of permanent warfare against Africa. The secret teeth of map-drawing, he says, is in the way those vertical lines called "longitudes" are drawn. Around the equator, and between the tropics of Capricorn and Cancer, the lines are more like straight lines with short distances between them. Beyond Capricorn and Cancer, they become curves and arches, thereby widening the distances between them. Africa, which lies between the two C's, looks smaller to the eye than Europe and North America, which in turn appear to the eye very much wider and spread out. The African child, in the classroom, is secretly indoctrinated into seeing his whole continent as smaller than Europe and North America, while the European and North

American child (USA and Canada) is brought up with a confidence that their lands (and therefore their peoples) are bigger and stronger than Africa. The hidden hints are for the African child to feel globally second-class while the North American child feels terrestially top-class. Mazrui also challenges the African geographer to confront the European convention that the northpole is where Europe and the Americas are while the southpole is where Africa is. Who, he asks, says that Europe should be sitting on top of Africa? Or rather, why should the African child be taught, by map makers, that his continent is the servant perpetually carrying Europe, a master-continent on its head? Put in the languages of Hollywood, why should the dashing, handsome (or beautiful), tough or good guys, heroes and heroines, in videos watched by the African child, be almost always a Caucasian white person? What silent war is Hollywood waging?

Opponents of Ali Mazrui always accuse him of going for what is intellectually shallow precisely because his insights burst across the consciousness of his listening victims with the bangs and flares of fireworks. His defense has always been that there are hundreds of thousands of very brilliant people out there inventing, manufacturing, and selling what fireworks are made from. And there are millions of others at mass celebrations who find fireworks exhilarating. The world of advertisements, for example, is rooted in the belief that flares tickle nerve centers in brains and pockets, to the merriment of bank accounts of millions of campanies worldwide. Even Soviet Communism couldn't fight American advertisements on Radio Free Europe.

And if Mazrui is right, where have all the creators of political imagination for Africans gone? Since 1200 A.D., Africans have been the target of successive European intellectual fireworks. Each season of European imagination has brought centuries of bleeding to Africa. From 1200 to the 1870s, Europeans invented (and with much satisfaction of greed) the deportation of millions of Africans from the eastern eyelashes of the Atlantic Ocean to its western eyelashes; from the 1860s to 1992, the European Community invented the Lome Convention and polished the cannibalistic teeth of their debt traps to effect a financial slavery, which is now sanitarily referred to as "total net transfers." From 1992 onwards, the political union of Europe, under the Maastrichts Treaty, brings with it the "pro-democracy recolonization of Africa" as well as the use of AIDS as a population pesticide across the African continent. The Debt Drain will justify recolonization as a "debt alleviation and effective performance mechanism" (to use IMF lingua). Europe in the past used debt collection to break Mohammed Ali and colonize Egypt, to colonize Liberia, to invade China. It is a game they know well.

But, all that is rather pessimistic and obviously liable to the charge of paranoia. Maastrichts, for example, has given birth to a most positive product of intellectual fireworks between "the North and South." A 1991 Maastricht Conference gave the world "The Global Coalition for Africa (GCA)." The marketers of this new product proclaim it as "a North-South forum that brings together African leaders and Africa's external partners." It collects and neatly packages "timely, accurate data" and subjects it to "rigorous analysis" in a mission of "assessing progress or lack of it" in Africa's crawl towards development. The practical goal is to keep "decision makers, North and South" well informed so that there can be "a consensus and (an) embarking on well-coordinated action to put Africa on a path to real sustainable development."[1]

There is optimism, drive, and generosity in all that. And a determination to market Africa's place in the global drama of decisions and resource-grabbing as competitively as Boris Yeltsin's cry to Capitalism to dash across the vastness of Russia and win the Economic War against yesterday's "radical Communists" who now (by the flick of a BBC tongue) are today's "conservatives." The sharing of duties is "global" (even if the billion-populated China is not represented). The Kruschevian troika of Sir Ketumile Masire (President of Botswana), Robert S. McNamara (Kennedy's brain-bomber of the Vietnamese people and also former president of the World Bank), and Jan P. Pronk (Minister of Development and Cooperation of the Netherlands) are the "Co-Chairmen." Their chief keeper of secrets (Secretary) is Dr. Boubakar Diaby-Ouattara (who apparently refuses to be identified as the first Executive Director of ECOWAS.

The troika is advised by a committee made up of ten African economic ministers; ten ministers from "donor countries"; a representative from the Organization of African Unity (but *not* its secretary general); one representative each from the African Development Bank, the Economic Commission for Africa, and the United Nations Development Program; the secretary general of the United Nations Conference on Trade and Development; the commissioner for Development of the European Community; the director of the African Department of the International Monetary Fund; the World Bank's vice-president for Africa; and the executive director of the United Nations Fund for Population Development. It is a galaxy of power. It may hint at odious glamours of Chief Lubengula, but it is probably no more than a mere whiff which a consistent and solid dose of goodwill on all sides can keep in check. While "ten African economic ministers" of beggar economies might seem a bit frail compared to "ten ministers from donor countries," the power of the pathos in a beggar's empty bowl has lethal potency inside the eyeballs of a donor minister.

The message of the "First Annual Report" of the GCA is brutal and frank. For example, Uganda (which Winston Churchill once ecstatically called "the Pearl of Africa') leads the continent (in 1991) in parting with 63 percent of her earnings from exports as the debt it pays to "donor countries." In 1991, Uganda received only two million American dollars as "foreign direct investment." In 1991, about 117 of her children (out of every one thousand) died. The figures for Guinea Bissau are 45, 0, 148; for Madagascar 44, 14, 114; Burundi 43, 1, 106; Cote D'Ivoire 40, 0, 95, and for Ghana 35, 20, 85. The comparative figures for "communist-conservative" China are 12, 3, 340, 28. Just one more horrible arithmetic. Africa, as a whole, paid debts to those generous "donor countries" to the terrible total of 12 billion American dollars in 1991 alone.[1] The generosity of a money-lender is at the moment of giving you his money, and not at the moment of coming with a truck to collect your debt payments.

Again, all this is rather negative, if not depressing. The explosive flare and power of fireworks is a matter for celebration. The ultimate lesson and historic duty of the "The Global Coalition for Africa" is its yelling out that it is about time there emerged a "coalition" *of* Africa, in an African Union Government, for African combat with the intellectual fireworks from other peoples' imaginations. The horrendous message that Uganda loses 63 percent of the monies earned by the coffee, tea, cotton, and groundnut peasant farmers of that "country of blood" (to prapharase one fo Idi Amin's key Minsters, Herny Kyemba) is clearly that it is no longer a viable state in world politics. Yet Uganda is still a land of promise (to quote a South African jornalist writing in 1961) because of its fertile lands and abundant rainfall—things which peasants, thank God, don't have to produce and give to "donor countries." Guinea Bissau, Madagascar, Mali, Chad, Niger, Senegal, Mauritania, Tanzania, Kenya, Botswana, etc. are not lucky. It is obviously time for a new imagination, an urgent imagination. It is time for these countries to commit "Sovereignty suicide" and become (in Nyerere's words) "more honorable each as an office cleaner in a Union of African States." Europe and the United States will oppose it. So will Russia (since it will upset the territorial balance of power, both in the Mediterranean Sea and the Indian Ocean geopolitical orders). And so what? The Portuguese were, and still are opposed to free Mozambique and free Angola, but that did not stop the sky from leaking into fascist Portuguese hearts. Let Union Government of Federal Africa be the collective imagination for realization *now*. It will be our worthy congratulations present to the tormented dreams and courage of the peoples of all races of post-apartheid South Africa.

Notes

1. *African Social and Economic Trends,* 1992 Annual Report of the Global Coalition for Africa (Washington, D.C., November 1992), Provides very useful data on the African condition.

7

TURNING OUR HISTORY
INTO MAD DOGS

We sat in his upper-class house in the Zamalek section of Cairo. Golden lionheads were the ends of armrests on his vintage chairs. An Oxford-educated economist, he had been a special advisor to President Nasser. The American Central Intelligence Agency (CIA) and other western European intelligence agencies, he had said, decided in 1967 to call Nasser's bluff by forcing him into the Six-Day War.

Since 1948, President Nasser, then a young military officer, had come to the conclusion that the Arab world could only defeat Israel if Egypt was industrially and militarily strong, because only Egyptians were willing to suffer the pain of defending Arab nationalism against Israeli Zionism. Other Arabs, especially their feudal rulers, liked enjoying life too much to have time for the inconveniences of a good fight. When the Free Officers Movement, led by Gamal Abdel Nasser, overthrew the corrupt British-puppet Government of King Farouk, Nasser persuaded the rulers of

Saudi Arabia, Kuwait, and the Gulf Emirates to annually pay for his military build-up against Israel. He used Radio Cairo to whip up Arab anger and pride from under these oil sheiks (by way of intimidating them with the nationalist fires of their own peoples). He sold the vision of Egypt as the sword of the Arab cause, and he himself as the new conqueror of Christian Crusaders in the modern Battle of Jerusalem.

The money flowed in, but Nasser and his advisors had other ideas. While buying the symbolic Arab bomber once in a while, he spent most of the money in civilian industrialization of the Egyptian economy. In the Egyptian pharmaceutical industry, for example, drugs were made, which were falsely labeled "Made in West Germany," then exported to distributors in Germany who in turn re-exported them to European, American, Asian, Latin American, and African markets. Egypt was at the edge of an industrial take-off. Israel and the west panicked.

Nasser, a charismatic man of high drama, translated each good news from his scientists and industrialists into more hyperbolic and misleading military rhetoric for the consumption of his audiences, the golden oil sheiks and their hungry mass publics. "He was going to drive the Jews back across the Mediterranean Sea"; "Arab military air power would blow out Israel to form a new anti-Zionist lake," etc. But, the CIA and Israel's MOSSAD spies would not be fooled. To stop Nasser's industrialization, they decided to drown *him* into the bitter lake of his own rhetorical showmanship and grand poetic bluffs: force Nasser to fight. And make the issue more dramatic by exposing his grand plan of diverting money meant for buying weapons (for which Western banks and industrialists would have loved him if he had done so) into more dangerous economic strength. And so, with dollars, they bought Nasser's Chief of Air Staff. When the Israeli planes arrived with their bombs, the Air Chief was flying over Cairo Airspace assuring his command that all was well that remained tame. His men missed the meaning of his Jewish Arabic. The point, however, was that the Arabic element in Egypt had been used by the Euro-Americans to bomb her future back into economic backwardness. The professional economist in our host wept in tears of Egyptian nationalism.

The next day Nevine El Shishini (working on instructions from a voice in Geneva) escorted me to the National Museum in Cairo. The designers of its exhibits meant to hit the visitor with the overwhelming Black African character of Egyptian heritage. The statues of the pharaohs, their guards, and their armies were screamingly Black Africans or "Negroid." The royal court women aristocrats and young girls were Black African women while their maids and servants were white Caucasians or brown Syrians. The men, captives of war, with terrible chains around their necks as they stood in long rows or being brutally slaughtered in war, were also white Caucasian. The hair styles of the Egyptian women were so very similar to those one had seen on women from Rwanda, Burundi, Nigeria, Senegal, and Zaire. Cobras with their necks spread out and eyes at permanent revolution stood out from above the heads of Pharaohs while claws of lions formed the feet of their beds.

At the pyramids Nevine, my guide, talked of how Napoleon on conquering Egypt had been so infuriated at the Black African face of the Sphinx that he had ordered French soldiers to break off the face. They only succeeded, thank God, in chipping off a small piece of the nose of the royal statue. His stubborn and contemptuous wide African lips merely looked on till today. An Egyptian joke says that foreign invaders come and go, but the pyramids reign over Egypt. The statue of the Black Pharaoh Rameses ll in central Cairo is simply awesome and magnificent.

Back at the hotel in Cairo, we were told another joke. It involved Presidents Nasser, Gaddafi, and Nimery. The three leaders came together down an elevator. It refused to open on touching the ground. President Nasser turned to Gaddafi and begged him in the name of the New Arab Revolution (which his youthful self now represented) to order the lift to open. Gaddafi did. The elevator refused to heed. Gaddafi turned to Nasser to use his old fire of Arab Nationalism to get obedience. The elevator refused to heed to Nasser. Whereupon Nasser and Ghaddafi turned to Nimery and said, "You are a visitor, perhaps it will obey you." Nimery said "open." It did. The joke had been told in answer to my question about why it was that the waiters and porters on the hotel were all dark-skinned persons. The elevator had answered President Nimery of Sudan because he was after all addressing his constituency in diaspora. We laughed with our host at the witticism in the joke. My companion, Hasu Patel, was a Zimbabwean scholar of Indian descent.

Egypt has, since President Sadat's time, decided to attract Western money with tourism to the pyramids. It was a form of revenge because from Moscow to New York individuals and museums have looted gold, silver, and stones, which Egyptians of the Pharaohs had used to create the most beautiful ornaments. They have been valued in trillions of dollars over the last century. Sadat felt that some of that money could return to Egypt with Euro-American tourists. Money is good for the Egyptian economy, but it is also a celebration of the Black African past of Egypt. The Arab element in Egypt delights at inventing and laughing at jokes about Black Sudanese waiters and menial workers serving in Arab Egypt, but not at the celebration of their ancestral genius. To make things worse, Sadat came from the South; from towards the Sudan. His hair, we were told, "was African." If the theories of Aristotle and of mathematics and architecture, which the Arabs had taken to primitive Europe between 1100 and 1200 AD, had come before that of the Pharaohs, all would have been well. But they did not. Arab nationalism catches indigestion from the Black African foundation of Egyptian nationalism.

The voice from Geneva had also persuaded Professor Boutrous Boutrous Ghali to receive us and treat us well. Or rather, to tolerate our enthusiasm. Into his office in *Al Ahram* Building we sat (that all-powerful newspaper of Mohammed Heikal, Nasser's window on the world). Boutrous Boutrous Ghali was a senior editor at the *Al Ahram* newspaper, as well as a professor of International Law at Cairo University. He pleaded poverty for his two hats. As a professor he was too poor not to need another job. That was one of the sacrifices which his class had to make in the service of Nasser's socialism. His credentials were formidable. Nasser had sent him to draft the constitution of the Organization of African Unity (OAU) and appointed him legal adviser on African affairs and the Non-Aligned movement. He was also the carrier of Nasser's midnight messages to all parts of Africa. Nasser had made him (a Coptic Christian intellectual and renowned legal scholar) an important actor in world affairs. He never told us this. Our "Deep Throat" informer did. It made us understand the mist that suddenly rose in his eyes when we told him what Nasser had meant for our young imaginations. He was the unspoken side of Nasser's Egyptian nationalism, which Islamic Arab nationalism at its most rabid and violent moments loved to blot out.

Somebody has been taking notes too on Egyptian history and its sense of humor. With the military taming of Ayatollah Khomeini (using the guns of Baghdad), then of Saddam Hussein (using in part the silence of Tehran and open hostility from Cairo), it is now Egypt's turn to be tamed, perhaps, with the use of the angry night wolves of Iraq and Iran. Anyhow, in a post-Cold War drama in which Israel is being asked to learn the art of kissing Arabs in broad daylight, with humane hearts, it is not unreasonable to assume that part of the bargain would be a wrecking of the Egyptian economy, civil peace, and political will and unity (with religious fratricide). The sight of Boutrous Boutrous Ghali at the pinacle of the United nations, and of thousands of Euro-American tourists coming to pay homage to Black African Egyptian genius of Ancient Egypt, are adequate baits to the IMF-tormented Arab and Islamic peoples. The media have recently carried stories of moslem fundamentalists killing scores of Coptic christians all over rural Egypt, as well as guns and bombs exploding inside buses and cafes used by European and American tourists.[1] The latest targets are Western banks and companies in Egypt. Our history becomes the mad dogs in our own houses, which are used by the enemy strategists to maul and eat us alive. Africa is being bashed.

In Zaire, Tshekedi is useful because he is from that legacy of "civilized educated Kasai Baluba evolves" who two years before independence pleaded with Belgium colonial officials and non-officials to treat them differently from the "primitive natives." The "primitives" include the vast Katanga, Equateur, and Bakavu regions, nine-tenths of the peoples and regions of Zaire. These are the peoples and regions whose aspirations Mobutu represents, even if catastrophically to date.

In Uganda, there was an ancient historical rhythm of "Northerners" coming South to fight as allies or infiltrate power-holders, overthrow them, and assimilate into them by adopting the languages of the people. It happened in Buganda, Bumyoro, Toro, Ankol, and Karagwe. The British distorted this process into recruiting only Northerners into their colonial armed forces while building their schools mainly in the South, for Southern children. The ultimate triumph of this permanent division of Uganda by the British was the tragic comedy in 1966 of "Northern" Colonel Idi Amin chasing "Southern" Kabaka Mutesa (King Fredie) into the wilderness of Rwanda and eventual death in exile among chuckling Britons in London. Museveni is currently back into that insane quagmire of North against South—politika Britannica on the equator.

In Nigeria, post-independence failures by Northern elites to deconstruct the negative sides of political and socio-spatial mobilities of earlier centuries (as part of strategic self- defenses within new global dangers) has been ignited (under their dozing eyebrows) at Zangon-Kataf, Tafawa Balewa, and all over Taraba State. Perhaps even more devastating and long-lasting is the IMF, the London and Paris debt collectors catching them still harvesting old attitudes of selfishness as a technology of power. The IMF, the Paris and London Club invaders are thus having such an easy run at utterly wrecking, impoverishing, morally bewildering, and destroying the communal ideology of the people's base around their "leaders." The message is simple, and urgent. We must re-tame and re-own our histories and harvest their dynamics for our own progress.

Notes

1. BBC broadcast on April 1, 1993, quoted a "moslem fundamentalist" as saying: "We will continue to attack the Tourist Industry in order to hurt this Government." A week before, there was an explosion inside the Giza Pyramid, one of the grandest monuments of Pharonic genius still in Egypt.

8

THE AFRICAN NOVELIST
AS A SPY

W. A. De Klerk in his historical novel, *The Thirstland,* makes
Louw du Plessis utter these words:

> These are the graves of our people. So we left them on the
> trek road. One can find them from here to Lake Ngami.
> And from Ngami to the Crocodile River in the Transvaal.
> From here to the Cunene; and beyond the Cunene to
> Humpata. They lie in the sand, in the limestone, in the
> bush .... Whether anybody will know them in ten years'
> time?.....Who can tell? The Lord had brought us a long
> way.....[1]

It is typical South African Boer morbid imagination. There is
suffering, death, and the shedding of their people's blood. They
are a people who celebrate dying on their feet because they are
marching—"trekking"—through bush and desert, running away
from anti-freedom (as incarnated by British colonial rule) to somewhere

and a better nowhere in particular. "The *idea* of trek, away from the present, away from the known," was long ago tamed into a philosophy.

But there is also a special gaze here; a vast geographical sweep over enormous territories, ranging from Transvaal to Namibia and beyond. De Klerk is complaining. The Berlin Conference of 1884-85, which shared out Africa to Europeans made heroes out of the explorers Livingstone and Stanley. But no one sings the praises of the peasant Boer explorers who traversed Africa from the Cape to the Transvaal, and then to Cunene River which borders Angola and Namibia. Yet why does he bring back the ghosts of Livingstone and Stanley who merely discovered that Africans had already discovered Africa because they started their burden of giving birth to mankind there?

De Klerk's novel was published in 1977 at the height of South Africa's invasion of Angola. This is a novel in the service of the politics of empire and foreign military adventure. The hero characters are hunters of elephants, lions, hippos, and ostriches. And they kill the Ovaherero, "Bushmen," Nama, etc., peoples who are defending their lands and sovereignty. The white man's gun is more powerful here than religion. The Boer has killed here before. He can and should kill again in the newly independent Angola.

The novel is set between 1878 and 1886. A group of peasant Boers leave their settled lives in the Transvaal. Why? "Freedom! We must trek...until we have found which is our own and will remain our own"—even if other African peoples already own such lands. They end up in Angola and settle in a place known as "Humpata on the High Serras." The historian, Basil Davidson, argued that a band of South African Boer immigrants did settle in a place close to where Savimbi's UNITA now has its ethnic base. Literature and politics have met in passionate trans-African and transhistorical embraces.

In September 1976, I was chasing geography and social contact on the Mona Campus of the University of the West Indies in Jamaica. As I turned the corner of a student dormitory, I suddenly heard angry voices. One had the sing-song twang of Jamaican talk, the other the staccato from the mental muscles of a West African. On gentle intervention, it turned out that the Jamaican student was on the prowl seeking to bully a "bushman African" who had swam seas to seek the educational and civilizing mercies of the Caribbean. The newly arrived Nigerian (and a Commonwealth scholar post-graduate student) was tolerating no such vulgar invasion of his peace. He seemed to calm down when I suggested that he was first and foremost an ambassador who must win back and not frighten away these hearts. I secretly wished that all those Africans, who since the 1800s had schooled in Europe, North America, Russia, and Asia, had written travel books, anthropological works, and novels for me and this young Nigerian to have read before our own huntings. The Nigerian was a student of English literature.

In May 1967, I had arrived at Accra on Swiss Air from Amsterdam. My mission was to wrench out from the National Union of Ghana Students (NUGS) grudging support for my plan to study military coups (including that which overthrew Kwame Nkrumah) as a killer of democracy in Africa. My report would be for the Research and Information Commission of the International Student Conference (ISC). They would fund it. As soon as I handed in my passport, however, I was declared a "prohibited person" and promptly put under detention (since it would be another four days before Swiss Air could put me on an exit flight). And what was my crime? Being a Hausa man from Northern Nigeria who had been recruited by Nkrumah (who was then in exile in Guinea) to be infiltrated into Ghana on a Uganda passport, for the purposes of organizing a counter-coup. "Being a Hausa Man!" But my Nigerian classmates had told me in Makerere that Hausa people are not milk people, not cattle folk! My confusion reached comic fever-point when on the second day in detention the immigration officer relented and confessed that Nkrumah was recruiting Hausa people from Northern Nigeria because they spoke the same language and physically looked the same as the Hausas from Northern Ghana! Well, I had by then read Achebe's *Things Fall Apart* and *Arrow of God*, Tutuola's *Palm Wine Drinkard*, the CPP's *Spark, Zik* and *Awo*, and none of them had prepared me for this Hausa trans-African espionage thriller. I wonder now if anything has since come out by way of promoting various Nigerian/Ghanian/Chadian/etc. foreign policy goals.

A final example. The Aboud military regime in the Sudan had decided on a program of diplomacy through sports. It sent a plane to carry a multi-sports team from Makerere Unitersity in Uganda to Khartoum. Our football team was a gallery of stars.

The goal keeper (John Afe) was the Nigerian Mid-West region junior keeper; the defense had a Kenyan and two Tanzanian (mainland) national team players. The attack had two Ugandan, Zanzibari, and Zambian national team players. It was therefore a culturally brave-eyed group, which was not intimidated by foreign travel and was determined to break all diplomatic padlocks our hosts put on *where not* to visit and *when not* to visit. And so it was that we invaded the Omdurman Central Market unannounced. A scuffle ensued, with white *jallabiyas* and reams of headwear furling and twirling. Voices slashed and splashed the air and soon swords sent glares into fears. By the time our silent spectators' pool was noticed, and tempers began unscrambling, it was rather late: but before blood was drawn. What was the problem? Nigerians! *There were over four million of them in Sudan.* We were aghast at this mathematical news. Our own post-graduate student from Ethiopia also added that there were "many Hausa people from Nigeria in Ethiopia who have been there for many, many, many years." Several years later, I read that fine novel by the Sudanese writer Tayeb Saleh , *Season of Migration to the North.* I was hoping that its hero was that West African immigrant in the Sudan. After all, somebody had claimed that President Nimeiry was descended from a Kanuri tribe in Nigeria (as shown by the cultural marks on his face). But Tayeb Saleh's book brought on other headaches to deal with. The literary potential for promoting consciousness of African unity through Omdurman remains ignored.

Anyhow, if De Klerk has urged for the need to celebrate the historical feats of geographical conquest by Boer peasants, hunters, and traders, surely the "discovery" exploits of African students abroad; Peul/Fulani cattle folk; the Hausa, Bambara, Wolof, Nupe, Mandingo, Ibo, Yoruba, Bangala traders, farmers, diamond, and gold smugglers, etc., across Africa and the globe deserve celebration too. For realizing, new political horizons.

In 1983, I marveled at the sight of the great novelist Ngugi wa Thiong'o walking down the central avenue in Dakar, the capital city of Senegal. A short man with a solid chest and a head that appeared heavy, he walked with his eyes glued to the pavement: allowing shafts of reality to reach him only through quick glances from corners of his eyes. Or so I imagined, and puzzled about this man whose writings (like that of the Caribbean-British writer V.S. Naipaul)[2] roared out with such wonderful verbal photographs of details from their settings. He told me of a terrible panic, which gripped him at Dakar airport when he suddenly found himself linguistically deaf in Africa (since he spoke neither French nor Wolof). Such cultural vulnerability, I thought, was a peculiar problem of the African elite marooned in school-bred colonial isolationism; which the Nigerian "discoverers" of Omdurman and Ethiopia, Fulani "explorers" of the vast lands from Futa Jallon mountains in Guinea (in West Africa) to Northern Tanzania (in East Africa), had for centuries learned to climb over and conquer.

But Ngugi also hinted at a new frontier. And, it is here that African ministries of foreign affairs as well as intelligence services really ought to come in. The novel, and other forms of the literary word, should begin to hold hands with the goals of foreign policy. The writer now should be funded to live and write in and of Brazil, in and of Japan and China, of North America, to research and write about our own "explorers" and "discoverers" of Africa (both ancient and contemporary). The best of Britain's novelists have been also some of her best spies. It is a disease worth catching. The Boer novelist, De Klerk, has already used it to bleed Angola.

Notes

1. W. A. De Klerk, *The Thirstland* (London: Rex Collings, 1977). "Our People are land-tamers, Karevapu," Botha said."They follow the sun; and they get where they want to be. They Know of Angola. That is enough." pp. 30–31.

2. V. S. Naipaul has done excellent literary work as travel portrayal of countries and societies. His book, *A Turn in the South* (1988), gives a penetrating picture of the ideological matrix of racial and social classes in the southern parts of the United States of America.

9

TIME FOR FOOD AND
POLITICAL IMAGINATION

Thanks to the ancient genius of the Somalis, we now know that
democracy is at rock bottom violence for the people, against the
people, and by some of the people. The British scholar Evans-
Pritchard had given notice of his glimpse of this phenomenon
while in the Sudan. He had learned to live in livid fear of a Nuer
laughter foaming out one moment, and abruptly molting into a
blood spill with the next wink of the brain. The jagged laughter
from one heart might pinch a tender groove in a nerve of another,
instantly twitching defensive muscles. Stems of flashing sticks
might clang out spurted furies. An unprotected head may jet out
blood as an injured *ego* calls out his *libido* to war in defense of
personal, family, and ethnic dignities (in that order of potency
and urgency). He called it "balanced antagonism" or each for the
defense of his freedom (and for all our freedoms, too). The colonial scholar in him would not let him salute his Nuer hosts of the

Sudan for founding a permanent cure against the emergence of a *Leviathan* and an Adolph Hitler.

The Somalis in our time, however, invoked the D of Democracy to combat and overcome the uniformed D of president Siad Barre's decades of bloody military dictatorship. It had all been latent in their clans and when gun sellers from other lands took a peep into their labyrinth of balanced passions, they rushed in with generous guns of war. By the time the rest of the world heard the terrible news, Somalis had been so busy at balancing blood for blood that they had all forgotten the Muazin's call to food. And television cameras soon turned starving skeletons from human participants in democracy to things of global horror, revulsion, and pity.

And no one else in Africa had apparently heard religious calls to producing food either. Take the countries to which God and European whims had parceled out the biggest chunks of Africa. The Sudan, with over one million square miles (the biggest of our lot), had, during 1979-1981, produced annual averages of "cereals, roots, tubers and pulses" measured at 186 kilograms for each citizen resident in the country. By 1988-1990, each citizen could only have (at least in the statistician's theory books) 139 kilograms. Cameroon had lowered her own rations for citizens from 348 kilograms to 312 kilograms. As in the Sudan, civil war had reduced generosity of Ethiopia's lands from giving out 228 kilograms per citizen to a mere 177 kilograms. The severest rebukes for these continental failures in agricultural fecundity were sent forth by Morocco and Egypt, countries to whom God had sent the Sahara locusts of sand dunes to eat away lands for agriculture. In the same years, Egypt increased her bounty to each citizen from 245 kilograms to 273 kilograms, while Morocco's filial bounty went from 231 to 357 kilograms. In far away China, where each All-China swallowing, each All-China up and down pumping of the citizen's esophagus, sends down one billion rations of food (almost three times that of simultaneous All-Africa swallowing), their production per capita had wisely climbed up from 446 kilograms to 464 kilograms.

In the 1960s, there had been much euphoric talk about Sudan becoming "the breadbasket of the Arab World." Perhaps therein lay the problem. Nobody noticed that this was a land of Gezira cotton, Shilluk cattle, Darfur gum arabic latex, and milk from Nubian camels, and not of baking bread. And that being "Arabic" was a tool for plaiting hairs of inferiority complexes among certain elites in Khartoum and not for fertilizing collective imagination for development. The desperation to be Arab is a leaking basket that will not carry irrigation waters even out of a patient River Nile. The Gezira irrigation cotton had been Britain's desperate reply to Yankee impudence (in refusing to export to imperial Britain her cotton soaked in exported African slave sweat), rather than a product of Arab mercantile genius discovering Manchester's textile mills as lucrative cotton-chewing camels. A century after Mahdist fury at a *jihad* against plundering European infidels had died down, the Nuer, Shilluk, and Dinka swamps on the Nile at Bahr-el-Ghazel have only gotten more crimson with permanent blood-setting civil wars. Civil wars, which have lasted (with minor holidays) from 1956 to present, are the only man-made swamp, which Sudanese national imagination has invented and nurtured as tribute to the Nile's unresting sense of duty to that weeping country. No one, it seems, can transcend the sounds of silence and pain, which agriculture for food has known in gigantic Sudan.

Down towards the equator is vast Zaire, a country cursed by the past imagination of a greedy European man (King Leopold) born in a poor Belgium, which was once dredged from under the mocking laughters of the North Sea. The viciousness and greedy grandeur of the Sea had translated in his dreams to grabbing limitless territory in the bowels of Africa, and torturing its wretched peoples with endless agricultural labor to produce exports and wealth for himself. The violence subsequently used by the Belgians for fuelling agriculture in colonized Zaire reportedly employed more policemen posted directly over peasant villagers to enforce compulsory crop plantings than all the policemen and soldiers used by the British for controlling India for three hundred years. The land became a torture chamber, a zone of unending violence, rather than of nourishment and historically accepted and cherished responsibility for feeding human fecundity and appetites. Little wonder that the moment of independence became the big bang which depopulated the land and married the country to new and highly fertile wives called urban slums. And so, since Independence on June 30, 1960, Zaire is still waiting for new rains of imagination to germinate a new agriculture based on enjoyed service to humanity.

"Mainstream" American storytellers enjoy celebrating agriculture as the midwife of their territorial growth. European immigrant farmers settled in the States of Oklahoma and the Dakotas; and Minnesota, Illinois, Missouri and Iowa. And the railroads hauled to them industrial products out of East-coast industries, while bringing back East the blessing of their marriages to new lands. Of course, the goldeaters rushed on to California and Oregon, and occupied the eastern eyelids of the Pacific Ocean long before the Russian bears in search of furs had began to roll too freely down from Alaska and tasted Mexican *tequila* (as the Vodka of the tropics). But, the rugged farmers still had to feed the goldrushers and their passions.

The indigenous peasant farmer in Africa has similarly explored, migrated, occupied, and quietly laid historical claim to the lands of Africa. But, the official propagandists do not sing his praises and political heroism as a conqueror of territorial frontiers. European land-grabbers in Kenya, Tanzania, Zimbabwe, South Africa, Namibia, Angola, Mozambique, Algeria, and Zaire accused him of economic idiocy and historic irresponsibility for sitting on fine fertile land and not using it to feed European humanity. They drove him out, called on starvation to charge him, his children, his wives, and his livestock higher taxes of hunger (by way of locking the chains of slave labor around his legs and neck). He returned to respectability with his gritted teeth and determination to bleed a lot for the cause of prolonged national liberation struggles. But, the cruel wills of international economic and political power have still denied him his promised rewards. In Algeria, he had by the 1980s turned to the calls of a frustrated and violent God. In the rest of Africa the peasants have become the permanently insulted, to whom colonial European officials (British, French, Portuguese, and Belgian) and post-colonial African officials are the same invading locusts, with the latter now often eating even the roots of his crops.

Hundreds of thousands of them have died in Somalia, Southern Sudan, Uganda, Ethiopia, Chad, and the Western Sahel before the locusts have been chased away, and before the rise of new elite imaginations in African agriculture. In the Sudan, Cameroon and Cote d'Ivoire, a new dreadful land disease was creeping in during the 1970s. The multinational company LONRHO was to produce sugarcane of vast lands in Southern Sudan and Cote d'Ivoire. So were other Southern African companies.

An American company, DOLE Transnational, found sweet lands in Cameroon for growing pineapples for export to sweet teeth in other continents. German companies would, by the 1980s, dry up the milk in udders in Nigerian nomadic cattle by flooding Nigerian urban throats with chemical German milk. American wheat would struggle to dredge out millet, sorghum, and maize from ancient Nigerian appetites. In the Southern Sudan, the discovery of huge deposits of oil began to urge for a strategy of religious and ethnic cleansing, if not extermination. In short, a new invasion by new locusts; talking of the cruel rise of Sugarcane Dictatorships.

And yet, we must not get tired and deadened by the horrible television pictures of starving Somalis. Rather they should be lightning flashes and thunder claps across the imaginations of African agriculturists, urging new angers but not debilitating collective shame, forcing doors of new political visions—especially that vision, which sees out stagnating lands as a common and collective heritage and as bridges over which to cross to the promised political frontier of African Union Government. For now, however, we should immediately go for an "African Food High Command," for purposes of preventing and effectively coping with more democratic starvation in future Somalias, Sudans, Ugandas, and Mozambiques.

10

SOVEREIGNTY FOR AFRICA'S MILLET, SORGHUM, YAM AND GARI

The newscaster on the only radio in the country struggled to find the politically vaccinated tone of voice. "There has been a serious accident at State House. The Prime Minister was having his lunch when a piece of meat accidentally got stuck in his throat. He was immediately rushed to hospital and is now receiving treatment. The medical professor who handled the emergency says that there is no cause for alarm. People should go about their normal business and refrain from spreading false rumors. All those wishing the Prime Minister a quick recovery may send flowers and get-well messages to the National Hospital." Africa uses laughter as a lubricant, cooking oil, and a hurricane lamp for crossing darkness of soul. And so it is that villages of voices at laughter promptly sprung up; many taking their hint from a taut screech they heard in the throat of the radio announcer. "What do you expect," said the frying pans among us, "when you give power to people whose mothers have *never* known the scent of meat!"

"It is his foolishness that made him marry a wife from among banana eaters. They have told her to kill him, put witchcraft in his food. Since when did meat sit in the throat of those who rear cattle? It is the wickedness of her and her people! When he recovers, he must get rid of her!" So bellowed the lubricators of our anxieties. "Foolish woman, if she had just sat on him with those big bottoms of hers, the meat would have shot out of his throat like a bullet. She only knows that she has them when he is knitting them!" So taunted, those who lit lamps across our anxious hearts. Our country had achieved political independence only one month before the "Meat in the P.M.'s Throat Affair." It is understandable that food thus gave our national dignity an early panic.

The most senior government minister came in to his official residence with three wives, with rare gustoes for geographical exploration. The houseboy (a pre-independence and transcultural veteran) showed them a room for washing bodies. "Washing bodies inside the house in a hot climate on the equator, eh!" they giggled. Inside this room lay a white gleaming trough. It was smooth and hard as teeth; stronger than rock. It was so wonderfully big. The houseboy said the European occupants before them had the habit of filling it with water and sitting in it for hours washing their bodies. "Mad people, these Europeans. Only they will wash their bodies with their own body filth," moaned the eldest wife. Promptly they reached a strategic decision. The bark of the roots of the thorn tree would be pounded, soaked in water, and the derived juice used to scrub the huge basin. A part would be dried and set to burn slowly inside this rare utensil (all night long). The herb has a terrible smell: wickedly pungent. That wicked smoking laughter of it all night would drive away the evil spirits in bizarre European practices. To top this ritual of Africanizing a European social ecology, the big bath tub would thereafter be permanently used for brewing millet beer. When word of this strategic victory was sprayed far and beyond by a culturally injured houseboy (by way of what he saw as a personal demotion through the profanation of his former European master's technology), the "civilized educated-in-England" national elite whipped the new political wind with laughters of disgust and dismay. Like the houseboy, they too felt desecrated by this terrible drag in the invading ways of "bush politicians." The will of millet beer had rudely rammed its way across gates to our

independence. Was it an act from a long simmering historic out-
rage in an ancient grain of the tropics? Would it triumph in our
post-colonial horizon?

Mr. Thornton, our British Secondary School teacher of geography lessons, had worked a threat into an act of caring and
pedagogic tenderness. He wanted us to score distinction grades
in the coming School Certificate Examination, which were manu-
factured by something called "Cambridge." Nobody told us that
Cambridge was a little village in England, presumably because
only colonized Africans had villages. Anyhow, Mr. Thornton had
a strategy of intellectual benevolence (some might say, dictatorship). It anchored on the crops Africa exported to Europe. That
was the core truth. Its shells were the countries in which the crops
grew so that "Africa could export crops to Europe." So, if it was
"coffee" we would write it on top of the paper and draw a line
under it. Below the line would then be written Kenya, Tanganyika,
Ivory Coast, Cameroon, Uganda, and Zaire. If it was "cotton" we
would write under it Sudan, Nigeria, Zaire, and Uganda. If it was
"groundnut" we would write under it Senegal, Nigeria, and
Uganda. Then, tea, sugar, rubber, palm oil, cocoa, gum arabic,
pyrethrum, and sisal, each would have the countries it owned so
that "Africa could export crops to Europe." Somehow, Mr.
Thornton successfully vaccinated us with silence against the erup-
tion of attacks of questions about why millet, sorghum, yam, cassava, and our wild fruits didn't also own countries so that Africans could also export them to Europe. Mr. Thornton had farmed
a blindness in us, which we all brought forward into our independence.

Somebody said "if you do not give the Sun water to wash his
face and cool his teeth, then beware of the stare in his eyes."
Over 10,000 years ago thePharaohs in Egypt grew wheat. They
spread its seeds all the way to Northern Nigeria, as well as to
Morocco on the Atlantic. Then into Europe, up the Danube River,
before the Sun sent down political Saharas in waves and waves
of invasions by barbarians ranging from Iran to Greece. Napoleon came too. By the time bread made from wheat enthroned
itself securely as the monarch of stomachs, which were building
the Industrial Revolution (Europe's version of the pyramids), no
one remembered Africa anymore as a granary of grain. In 1845,
Sir Robert peel tore open the gates of England's Corn Laws, thus

instantly turning British stomachs into bottomless silos for grains shipped from all corners of the world.

Men of money, who saw grain as the "currency of currencies," swam seas and oceans to steal lands in the pampas of Argentina; slaughter Indians and buffaloes to rot and fertilize the prairies from Iowa to Manitoba, and from Illinois to Sacremento Valley in California. They stole the ancient wheat seeds of India to give agrarian fecundity to short winters in the Americas. By 1898 alone, the golden shine on American exports of wheat and flour was worth two hundred (200) million dollars. And no one heard the hungry silence over grains in the Sahara; beyond the shadows of the Egypt's pyramids; above the labyrinth of underground rivers beneath the Sahara. The slave trade had murdered African agriculture for over four hundred years.

By the 1880s, the passenger fares on ships paid by grains of wheat, corn, barley, and their flours declined steadily "so that distance became a minor factor in the cost of wheat." And England ate; and Europe ate more and more bread and biscuits, and Italian pasta. By 1884/1885, the year of the Berlin Conference of stabbing Africa with a million stab wounds and total tatoos of colonial boundaries, the city of Minneapolis alone "produced five million barrels of wheat flour." In short, Europeans came to Africa (by 1900) with after-dinner belches; looking for only snacks. Europe came to Africa with its pants tight around her bottomhole, leaking no hunger with which Africa's millets, sorghums, yams, cassava, grasses, and fruits could wag her will.

It is little wonder that Europe compelled out of Africa only the looting of rubber, ivory, tea, cocoa, tobacco, sugar, gum arabic, cotton, sisal, etc.; "the superfluous luxuries for which the rich would pay"; the leisure "foods" whose absence would ignite no political revolutions in European cities. The "crops Africa exported to Europe" with which Mr. Thornton, our geography teacher pulverized our teenage wits into putrid silences, were politically harmless in his Europe because the mass populations did not need them for basic survival.

Now the IMF is bringing a new silence over Africa's millets, sorghums, yams, cassava (gari), grasses, and fruits. It is being done in two ways: with the *wheat invasion* and promotion of African stomachs into colonized silos for bread mode from American wheat. After conquering and occupying Japan after 1945, the Americans had conducted the wheat invasion of Japanese tastes by targeting school children. It worked very well. It is also being done with the vigorous return to the old European colonial appetite for "export crops" and silence over millet, sorghum, yams, and cassava. The agricultural issue of the 1990s and beyond must—for Africans—be the establishment of the Sovereignty of her millets, sorghums, yams, and cassava. They must also become Africa's hunting horns for prying open stomachs and pockets of the rich Euro-American populations. If we can drink Coca Cola, they too can drink Kunu, Pap, and Gari. The *lex talionis* must now become "a gulp for a gulp."

The American beef cow eats seven pounds of grain (corn) in order to put on one pound of meat. American chickens eat two pounds of corn to put on one pound of meat. In Africa, the Fulani, Masai, Shuwa, Tocoleur, Shilluk, and Dinka cow loses ten pounds of meat while wandering in search of one pound of grass. We are yet to see our cattle, sheep, goats, local chickens, and pigs as buyers of our millets, sorghums, cassava, and yams. And yet, millions are desperately choked with absences of milk and meats. The call to a food revolution is obviously urgent. And action must be anchored on dreams of new and enhanced roles in world history for Africa's millets, sorghums, yams, and cassavas. As the United States of America and Russia reach out to settle on Jupiter and Mars, we too must reach out—to tap waters from a tapestry of rivers underneath the Sahara Desert, for turning her sands and barren empty faces into rivers of grains.

11

DEMOCRATIC POLITICS AND DECOLONIZING ACADEMIC RESEARCH IN AFRICA

> One form of neo-colonialism, notorious because it is not
> readily apparent, is perpetuated through the business of
> "aid," which dominates the vocabulary of economic poli-
> cies and plans of client African governments. Aid politics
> and practices have provided the justification for turning
> Africa into every donor's laboratory and the Africans into
> guinea-pigs for endless schemes of dubious researchers
> and charlatans of all kinds.

This rather muscular opinion is from a 1992 publication of the
Dag Hammarskjold Foundation, an institution not known for dis-
playing Marxist anger, let alone distributing it liberally to the Third
World. The title of the publication is daring in its apportioning of
blame for an allegedly African disease: *The State and the Crisis
in Africa: In Search of a Second Liberation: Report of the Mweya
Conference in Uganda, May 12–17, 1990.*

The condemnatory slant against "The State" in Africa explains the choice of the post-Idi Amin, post-Obote 2, and post-Okello regimes in Uganda. Yoweri Museveni's Uganda, the report says, "offered the example of an alternative to the notorious practice of military coups d'etat in Africa, that of ordinary people taking up arms to overthrow an unpopular regime and setting up a government of their own." That assertion is dubious on two counts. First, Museveni was no "ordinary" person. He was one of the rare breed of young Ugandans who got their view of world history and the role of the African man in it, from that legendary and revolutionary historian, Walter Rodney. He was lucky not to have come to study in Makerere, but instead went to the University of Dar-es-Salaam. If he had come to Makerere, he may well have become yet another victim of its organized intellectual suicides through silence over the true history of the African Man and Woman.

Perhaps more crucial to Museveni's political growth was the existence of the African National Congress (ANC), South West African Peoples Organization (SWAPO), The Front for the Liberation of Mozambique (FRELIMO), and the popular Movement for the Liberation of Angola (MPLA). All these organizations were represented in Dar-es-Salaam by real men and women with real-life experiences of political oppression, economic deprivation, racial domination and humiliation, of fathers, mothers, brothers, sisters, children, or friends killed or brutalized in their countries. Above all, Dr.Nathan Shamuyarira, later a minister in Mugabe's government in Zimbabwe, encouraged and arranged for FRELIMO to take Museveni inside Mozambique and show him the conditions in the areas which FRELIMO had liberated from the Portuguese colonial authorities. Dr. Shamuyarira was to edit a book of research essays by some of his students. Museveni's essay was on the application of the theories of Frantz Fanon to the liberation struggle in Mozambique.

The Dag Hammarskjold Foundation report is also silent on the fact that the fighters of the various liberation movements had been also in their own words "ordinary people taking-up arms to overthrow unpopular regimes." It was their thoughts, feelings, sufferings, victories, and confidence in their own futures, which had been Museveni's most important political school of life. Finally, the main thrust of the report ignores the tenacity and collective resolve shown by peoples in Zimbabwean Mozambique,

Angola, and Namibia to defend the freedoms they have won through the use of *"The States"* they have seized from colonialism.

But enough of criticism. The report has important things to say. For example, it asserts that "it is an embarrassing paradox that African governments officials usually find themselves talking only to foreigners about the continent's development . In only a few countries do government engage in public debate about development priorities with their own citizens." It is a polite way of saying that many African elites are victims of racial psychological poisonings, whose symptoms are called "inferiority complexes" and which are manifested as yearnings for the gratifying impulses of being confirmed by the other dominant race. Once, as an undergraduate a Stanford University the authorities summoned me to be in the entourage of visiting government minister of an African country. I was utterly confused, alarmed, and infuriated by the collapse of the carriage and discourse of "our African leader." It is probably little wonder that under such social chemistries many contracts and "aid agreements" were signed by such ministers many civil servant all over the continent, which are now killing millions in Africa through the effects of debt repayments.

There are more constructive recommendations in the report. For example: "the institutional and political infrastructure that encourages the development of new ideas, and subsequent inventions or innovations has not been built or sustained in Africa." This is not surprising. *The New Nigerian* for Saturday, April 17, 1993, carried a most perceptive essay by the late Malam Aminu Kano on the history of public policy-making in colonial and immediate post-colonial Nigeria. Under colonialism, Malam said, the British turned innovative planning into a racial monopoly. The African clerk and successor civil servants learn only the routines of moving files from desk to desk. As for the military, Malam said, "members of the Armed Forces are not astute politicians." When, after January 15, 1966, the civil servants and the military were left to themselves by the booted-out politicians, paralysis in major areas of public policy reigned supreme. Those who had been shielded away from policy innovations and creativity, and trapped in the ghettos of bureaucratic routines, obviously needed time to learn the craft of inventiveness and to develop the appreciation for the necessary infrastructures for it. In this regard, it is not altogether clear that African politicians, whether in government, opposition, or under silences imposed by the military have faced up to the need for policy think-tanks, or what the report calls "institutional and political infrastructure that encourages the development of new ideas." The Nigerian press claimed that the 1992 presidential primaries cost the banned candidates ten billion Naira. There is no mention that part of that staggering bill went into the setting up of lasting SDP and NRC policy-generating infrastructures. Both Nkrumah and Nyerere set up "ideological institutes" for party cadres, but nothing seems to have grown beyond them into even Third World variants of the American Heritage Foundation, the Rand Corporation, and The Global 2000, which produced Clinton.

"By broadening the basis for inputs into the policy process and by ensuring high-quality work from scientists and intellectuals, the prospect of developing more realistic and achievable targets may be enhanced." So says the report. This raises one immediate question for democratic electoral politics, in Africa. When Bill Clinton talked himself hoarse during his campaign typhoons, *Time* magazine opened the curtains to reveal which "wiz kid," or brilliant Rhodes Scholar, or professor had done the research and the computer calculations behind his promises, and punches of Bush. At the height of electoral political drama in the biggest democratic political area in Africa, the Nigerian politicians are reported to be locked up in auctioning alliances, votes, ministerial portfolios, etc., while apparently totally ignoring the academics in the institutions of knowledge, including seeming indifference to threats of strikes and closures in these institutions. The firsts secretary in the American Embassy in Pretoria, while on visit to Zaria in 1990, confirmed that in protecting apartheid, the South African regime had not only banned books it considered subversive from the rest of Africa and the world, but also virtually killed all research about the rest of Africa. There is probably a touch of exaggeration in the report, but the central message sounds familiar all over Africa. A politics which fears academic and policy research can only enjoy the merit of hollowness and irrelevance to the momentum of the rest of the world.

The report has a small mitigating suggestion to offer: "One possibility could be the creation of a consultative assembly, made up of representatives of different layers of society, to discuss strategies for achieving a second Liberation...." A brutal retort to this could be that a consultative assembly of the blind is not going to produce a plan for road maps. Dag Hammarskjold, as secretary general of the United Nations, was blinded by his hatred for Lumumba; Lumumba was blinded by his fury at the reluctance of the United Nations Security Council to force Belgian-invading troops out of his country as well as stopping Tshombe's secessionist rebellion in Katanga; the French mercenaries, together with their Belgian, South African, and Rhodesian pals were blinded by their hatred of Hammarskjold and killed him and Lumumba. Political passions and economic greed swamped the absent voice of academic research, as well as that of informed officials like Connor Cruise O'Brien. Having said all that, the message that Africa now needs a continental democratization of discourse over public policies, including the integration of the politics of democracy with sincere and patriotic academic hard work in research, is obviously pertinent and patently urgent.

For this to be of any benefit, however, it must first reject the current culture of "consultancy hawking" of the same data and recommendations that have flourished under the current hegemony of World Bank and IMF consultants. This virus of intellectual mercenarism and fraud has caught many African academics and resulted in the colonization (by the World Bank and the IMF) of some of the best brains in Africa and elsewhere in the Third World. These bodies pay high fees in strong foreign currencies and therefore dictate what issues are to be researched, which to be falsified by doctored research, and which to be killed with silence. This situation cannot, however, be permanent if political parties decide to liberate these colonized brains by rewarding them well within their own think-tanks, or (to use those nice long words again) within "institutional and political infrastructures that encourages the development of new ideas...."

12

CIVIL SERVANT OR
EVIL SERVANT?

"The worst enemies of this country are civil servants. If privatization and commercialization is to succeed in this country, we must first begin with privatizing the civil service." Those are the angry words of an academic who served as a State Commissioner during the Babangida regime (1985-1993) in Nigeria. A day after he spoke those words, the *New Nigerian* of May 4, 1993, reported Governor Dabo Lere of Kaduna State as fuming that "the staff of the revenue board, in collaboration with banks and other unpatriotic people," have been siphoning "into private pockets" whatever they collected for Kaduna State. He also claimed that if the situation were not stopped it would "grow out of proportion and will lead to the inability of government to provide even a single social service to the citizenry, which is unacceptable." A typical populist threat from a politician with his eyebrows twitching at the mass electorate out there. *The New Nigerian* also carried two other interesting stabs at public servants.

Chief M.K.O. Abiola, while introducing Ambassador Baba Gana Kingibe as his SDP running mate, also snapped the whip at civil servants. Said Abiola, "in a situation where square pegs were put in round holes in government appointment, no positive result could be expected." The other story is that a former French Socialist prime Minister, Pierre Beregovoy, had committed suicide by shooting himself in the head, because he "had been deeply affected by allegations of corruption arising from an interest-free loan of one million francs made to him in 1986 . . . (which he used) to buy a flat. . . ."

Beregovoy outdid the Director General of the British Broadcasting Corporation (BBC), who was caught paying virtually no taxes on his BBC income. Calls by his staff for his resignation were stoically smiled over by his employers. The Italians, too, have been engrossed in a political carnival of police arrests of top politicians for corruption and dealings with the Mafia. With the collapse of the Soviet Union, the United States and other Western European governments, apparently took the decision that the Mafia were not going to replace the Russian Communists as the new terror in the post–Cold War era. Not only were the Mafia destroying the youth with drugs they transported from Asia and South America, they were also destroying the civil services of countries (including the police) with bribes, threats of assassinations, sexual whitemail, as well as economic infiltrations of banks, real estate companies, etc. The Italian roots of the International Mafia have to be destroyed—by attacking Italian officials and politicians, their protectors.

In other lands, the Civil Service has come under attack from different sources. An American study done in 1990 states that the World Bank is angry. In the years 1947 to 1985, it loaned out the huge sum of 11 million dollars for various countries to construct and run irrigation projects. The results were disheartening. The trouble started with the Euro-American Companies that used the World Bank as their salesman. These companies put pressure on engineers (who designed such irrigation projects) "to focus on the design of physical works while ignoring social infrastructure, and to focus on larger, rather than smaller, projects."[1] In other words, make sure that the use of huge bulldozers, pumping equipment, canals, sprinklers, consultants, etc. give these companies as much opportunity as possible to export their capital equipment. World Bank experts came under pressure from these same companies to "overestimate benefits" and "underestimate...costs of sustaining" such irrigation projects. Other "experts" in the mentalities of Africans, Asians, and Latin Americans, advised on how always to talk down at their officials, to invoke old colonial inferiority complexes. If that failed, offer them bribes so that these contracts can be signed.

In Somalia, a new twist came into the science of bribing civil servants. A dam was to be constructed on the Jubba River. Someone hinted to top civil servants that with that inside information they could provide funds for them to buy large tracts of land in the areas targeted for irrigation. A "land rush" began, which some claim may have been the beginnings of the civil war, which has brought so much agony to that country. The civil servant had become the evil servant. Under President Ronald Reagan, U.S. government officials in several ministries, including Housing, Urban and Social Services, pocketed billions "of the taxpayer's money" while clever young men became overnight billionaires by manipulating trading in shares on Wall Street. The Pentagon or Defense Department excelled in corrupt overpricing of contracts. Paradoxically, it was the Reagan regime which led the most vicious attacks on "government bureaucracy"—meaning civil servants in other countries, including Africa.

In Africa, the attack on the civil servant had taken place in two earlier phases. In the 1960s, the enthusiasm by nationalist politicians to bring health clinics, schools, roads, seeds, or "development" coincided with the African civil servant's new freedom to aspire to the very top (in the future), as well as to sit (right now) on the chairs and desks which formerly had been the monopoly of white European colonial officials. Some politicians were exhilarated by the sensation of giving dictations to a white woman secretary, as they revolved around on their new big chairs. In the context of post-colonial European bitterness at losing empires, and fears of Russian communists wooing away angry nationalist politicians, the strategic decision was taken to disrupt this African drive for development. The colonial soldier was urged to use his gun and expose the nudity of the African civilians in power. Military coups were the "order of the day," from the death of President Olympio in Togo in 1961, to Milton Obote's overthrow in 1971. In Nigeria, it resulted in a most destructive three-year Civil War, and a derailed nationalism. In Uganda, it destroyed perhaps one of the few *uncorrupt* regimes in Africa as well as producing one of the most brutal decades from one country, which had achieved such a high level of material development. In Sudan and Zaire the gun had remained a hungry Dracula for over thirty years now. Some say that the African civil servant tasted corruption under these military regimes.

The second attack on an alliance for development between the African civil servant and the African politician came with the victories of liberation movements in Mozambique, Angola, Zimbabwe, and Namibia. This alliance was even more frightening to the Euro-Americans. The civil servants, politicians, and soldiers, in FRELIMO, MPLA, ZANU-PF, and SWAPO liberation movements had fought and suffered for power together under socialist and nationalist ideologies. The Soviet Union, China, Algeria, Cuba, Nigeria, North Korea, etc., had given them all diplomatic, moral, and military weapons. Allowing the civil servants, politicians, and soldiers in these countries to settle down and succeed was a veritable nightmare to the NATO countries. Countries like Brazil and South Africa dreaded television pictures of Black peoples defeating and humiliating white peoples. Their own Black populations might do the same *tonight*! And so, it came to pass that RENAMO and UNITA have been invested, funded, and supported by European and Brazilian governments and mercenaries to this very day. The tenacities of these liberation-movement regimes is a grand and historic monument to human freedom.

But, back to the World Bank and its new-found anger with civil servants in Africa, Asia, and Latin America. In India or Pakistan, we are told of those vile "water gate operator(s) who stay in a nice, dry office during the monsoon season rather than doing his assigned work....The operator is paid but does not do the work that is supposed to be done." His bigger bosses, in the faraway offices, in the capital cities have their vilenesses, too. For example, in India, about nine million dollars was spent in constructing Jamuna irrigation project. But "five years later, less than a third of the planned service area was receiving irrigation water." The officials did not steal money, but the local farmers refused to construct field canals because throughout the conception, planning, construction, and completion of the project no one had ever consulted them and sought their wisdom. Top civil servants, we are told, suffer from a mental illness known as "top-downism." They do the thinking and "drawing up rules and guidelines" while those who benefit from such brilliance only obey orders and instructions handed down to them.

The irony in this accusation against top civil servants is that their tormentors, the "World Bank experts," do exactly the same thing to them. They are talked down to, if not brutally abused by American and European boys "who are often the same age as their own children." If Governor Dabo Lere of Kaduna State is infuriated by theft in his revenue division, then the World Bank experts must have reams of computer data on corrupt civil servants, which then give them more gusto for talking abuses at their beggars. And this is before the peculiar Nigerian element of setting official buildings ablaze to cover up corruption is added into the picture.

Professor John Armstrong, in the mid-1970s, published a major work on the historical social chemistry for producing top civil servants (he called them "elites") in Britain, France, and West Germany. A core factor he found in all three histories was their peculiar education from childhood to university graduation. That education increasingly was carefully crafted to produce the qualities of commitment to the burdens of statecraft. Certain institutions of learning, from elementary to university education, built into the experiences to which they exposed their students certain vital ingredients of personality and intellectual development particularly suited for statecraft. The names of Eton, Harrow, Sarah Lawrence, Oxford, Sorbonne, etc. were locations of social chemical industries. Armstrong was a little shy about the question of the wealth which the parents needed to get their children in and through, but it was taken for granted.

I went to Stanford at the level of a sophomore (or second year) undergraduate. I was officially housed in a "fraternity house" for the "best and the brightest." Gary Messenger, for example, had won the best national undergraduate history essay competition for three years in a row. The Japanese final-year student in architecture beat all the firms from all over the country, which tendered for a Stanford project, etc. My own war became one of showing that the Black kid is a real BB (Black and Brains). But, my yearmates had been put through earlier experiences beginning from the age of ten years (in 4-H Clubs, summer camps, Boys Brigades, attendance at Stanford Abroad campuses in France, Austria, England, etc.; serving as research assistants of congressmen and senators in Washington, D.C., etc.) which my colonial primary and secondary school education had not offered me. I had played cricket, football in the first eleven up to University, a little lawn tennis, and boyscouting. But that was it . And nobody among my African and British teachers ever talked to me about becoming a future carrier of the burden of statecraft. At Stanford, I was in the campaign strategy team for the election of a Democratic Party candidate for the Student Union leadership, against the Republican Party candidate. The team decided on inviting Vice President Hubert Humphrey to visit Stanford and improve the visibility of our candidate.

All the other members of our campaign team had done "door-to-door" distribution of Democratic Party campaign material in their home states since their days in secondary school. Vice President Humphrey shook my hand, and I recalled with a pinch of anger that I had never been taken that seriously in my own country. So, what is the point of all this long tale? Perhaps it helps in answering an angry question, which was once bluntly put to the Cambridge, Oxford, Harvard, Yale, etc. products (who have been in positions of power in Nigeria) why they had let the country grind into despair and confusion. Going to these places to read books and wear gowns when you had already shaved your first beard before you left Nigeria (or Africa for that matter) is not the same thing as undergoing all the other social rituals crafted for preparing you for final fruition in those universities. Perhaps the underdevelopment of the social chemistry for producing the civil servant of Africa (and not evil servants of Africa) needs much more thought and imagination.

Chester Barnard wrote a classic work on public administration. He insisted on crafting motivating forces or "incentives" for a bureaucrat. Some incentives are material—like having a personal office without cobwebs for curtains; going down in a lift to a car park in the basement and driving home instead of walking and wearing rain into your home; having money to buy what you want without whispering to the trader that this will be your last takeaway on credit, etc. Other incentives, he said, are psychological and moral—such as, respect from your peers for your excellence; patriotism; following the best moral injunctions of your religion; a feeling that you are involved in something grand and not mere petty rituals, and bashings from those irked by racist, tribal, or inferiority complexes, etc.

Chester Barnard was writing for a developing and aggressive American industrial economy. He ignored colonial inferiority complexes, which pervaded aspects of Harvard, for example, which made professors of literature teach only British authors and none of the American writers. Young men like Bill Clinton felt that they needed the tag and gown of a Rhodes Scholar from Oxford, in England, for their future political aspirations. Stanford publicly referred to itself as "the Harvard of the West," while the universities in the heartland of the country such as Chicago, Northwestern, and Wisconsin (Madison Campus) recruited most of their staff *from* Harvard, Yale, Princeton, and Cornell as a way of wearing the aroma of excellence. But, there was also a fundamental pragmatic basis for this. It was the way to guarantee recruitment into the elite class of the American Federal Civil Service whose mandarins mostly came from these "ivy league" universities .

The claim has been made that the Civil War in Nigeria (1967–1970) and the Oil Boom (1970–1980) turned Nigerian public officials from a civil service in to a selfish evil service. They saw contracts for importing war material make millionaires of politically "well-connected" individuals. Then they saw the "Cement Invasion" make more millionaires. Then, the contracts for road construction made still more overnight millionaires. Finally, some people began to be allocated oil, a public property, for export as easy individual roads to millionaireships. Something inside the civil servants cracked and began to leak out ponds, then pools, and later oceans of "you chop, I chop" attitudes and behaviors. The scenario appears convincing, but it begs that simple question: Did Nigeria ever have a civil service before 1960? Were the colonial and native authorities, the emirs or chiefs-in-council, their district heads down to their ward heads ever servants of civil society and the public interest? If you ask historians of NEPU politics, such as Alkassum Abba, and politicians like Gambo Sawaba, their answer is a definite "No, never." NEPU's politics was, they will tell you, a struggle to give Nigeria her first civil servants; her first officials who knew the conditions of the people, their sufferings, their aspirations, and committed themselves selflessly to transforming terrible poverty; to give them dignity and happiness.

So, where do we go from here, not only in Nigeria, but in Congo, Kenya, Togo, Senegal, Uganda, Somalia, Algeria, Sudan, etc., where the civil servant is now under attack? The Dag Hammerskjold Foundation in a 1992 publication, even called for a "second liberation" of the public interest against the civil servant (whom they call the "State"). My angry former State Commissioner friend has called for the "privatization of the civil service." The *New Nigerian* of May 4, 1993, quotes M.K.O. Abiola as saying that "the next civilian administration should be run like business enterprises and that bureaucracy would have to go." Very bellicose words. I can hear the civil servants or "bureaucrats" smiling and sharpening their wits for war.

Perhaps the answers we seek are in the pockets of headmistresses and headmasters of schools, provosts of polytechnics and colleges of education, vice-chancellors and registrars of universities and their equivalent teachers and academics. What social chemistries are *they* crafting for turning their wards into servants of the public interest? What have successive vice-chancellors and senior administrative staff crafted at Ahmadu Bello University, which makes their graduates different from those out of the Universities of Ibadan, Nsukka, Benin, Jos, etc. in providing service to civil society, instead of being mere selfish evil servants? The same questions go for the academic staff. Is it enough that one be a professor to become a vice-chancellor, or must we begin to ask candidates what visions they have for a university that will produce leaders of society into the twenty-first century?

13

OLIVER TAMBO,
JIMMY CARTER, AND
MIKHAIL GORBACHEV

An unnamed contemporary of Nelson Mandela told *Sechaba* a
most interesting and profoundly human as well as South African
story. The African National Congress had taken the decision to
evolve from non-violent protests and demonstrations (against
apartheid with its political dictatorship, economic exploitation,
and deliberate impoverishment of the Black, Indian, and Colored
peoples) into armed struggle. The South African police had em-
barked on a nation wide mass hunt to capture Mandela, who had
gone underground. One night, the ANC executive who had cho-
sen Mandela as their commander-general held a secret meeting.
Mandela was ordered to go and inform ANC agents and units in
certain locations. It was now midnight. Dressed as a chauffeur,
Mandela ran into a heavy police roadblock. There were cars
ahead of him being searched. Suddenly, a policeman left the
others and came to search him and his car.

He came round to the driver's side again, and very delib-
erately, put his head through the window so that he could
peer directly into the face of the driver. Holding this position, he asked him what he was doing and where he was
going. Then, suddenly, his expression changed, a sign of
recognition appeared in his eyes, his stern expression
turned into a slight smile. Without waiting for a reply to
his question, he pulled his head out of the window, looked
ahead to where all the other policemen were still busy,
looked back at the tense Comrade Mandela, and tersely
said, "Quickly go round and past the side of the other ve-
hicles—don't wait." With that, he signalled the policemen ahead to lift the barrier and let the car through immediately.[1]

The unnamed elder who told this story may well have been Oliver
Tambo. The story has all the major ingredients of the history of
the African National Congress—the daring, the creative adapt-
ability of its leaders; the ferocious use of white state police to
hunt them down like animals; the white determination to kill Black
political demands for power by cutting off the heads of their leadership—but above all the essential political and revolutionary potential of each individual Black and white, peasant, lawyer, 'mine
worker, and policeman.

The African National Congress was founded on January 8,
1912 by the coming together of the common will of precisely
such a polyglot of people. At Mangayng (Bloemfontein), del-
egates came from all over Southern Africa "They included," we
are told, "workers, farmers, peasants, professionals, journalists,
traders, churchmen, chiefs, members of African royalty, poets,
musicians, authors." One hears here later, echoes of the "mother
of African music," Mariam Makeba, and Dennis Brutus, Ezekiel
Mphalele, Ruth First, etc. It is these two legacies of the political
relevance for the liberation struggle of all social strata in South
Africa that Oliver Tambo carried with him into exile when the
ANC leadership directed him to leave the country and build the
armed struggle from outside South Africa.

One of the founding fathers of the ANC, Pixley Seme, made a
prophetic statement in 1906. He said: "The regeneration of Africa means that a new and unique civilization is soon to be added
to the world."

Oliver Tambo died 87 years later, before the final end of apartheid whose beginnings prompted Seme's statement, but perhaps they had already fulfilled a major part of Seme's promise.

Five years after the founding of the ANC, the world was shaken to its very foundations by the birth of its first socialist state, the USSR, in 1917. The new and unique state was, for seventy years, to play a most significant part in the political fortunes of the ANC. The USSR's growth into a military and economic superpower put into world history a shoulder from which peoples oppressed by capitalist empires could not only stand and shout abuses at their tormentors, but by the 1960s (in Mozambique, Angola, Zimbabwe, Namibia, and South Africa) fire rocket launchers at Portuguese, Rhodesian, and South African troops, tanks, and aircraft bombers. To commemorate its 70th birthday, the ANC National Executive Committee under Oliver Tambo's leadership could boast openly that "The peoples of Africa, of Southern Africa and of South Africa are not alone. We too have our allies and loyal friends—countries and peoples who share the same vision as we do, who recognize that all humanity is diminished and world peace and security threatened by the continued existence of the apartheid regime. We greet the governments and peoples of the Socialist Community of nations...."

Oliver Tambo set out to add the "new and unique civilization... to the world" by conquering the world community by turning it against apartheid. His chief weapon was lifted directly out of the heart of the ANC, the belief in the revolutionary potential of each and all peoples. Chris Child, the trade union secretary of the British Anti-Apartheid Movement, gave the following report of their activities in 1981. That year, he reports, the National Union of Public Employees "denied rehearsal facilities to choirs, which planned to sing in South Africa; in Birmingham, the trades council started a campaign against the recruitment of unemployed car workers by the South African Sigma Company; demanded that schools, local authorities, and workers canteens should not use South African goods; other trade unions gave support for Black workers in South African goods; other trade unions gave support for Black workers in South Africa who were sacked (by British companies, such as Leylands) for engaging in trade union strikes; etc." All these seemed minor and trivial. After all, Britain, to use Oliver Tambo's own words, "is the source of our misery in Southern Africa." Moreover, in 1981, over twenty thousand

British workers had emigrated to South Africa to go and enjoy the loot of Black oppression. But the British Anti-Apartheid Movement was urged by the ANC to try and try again to secure the support of the British workers to give moral, political, material support for the liberation movements in South Africa and Namibia."

Oliver Tambo went to Jamaica, on the invitation of the Jamaican Workers Party as part of their celebration of Nelson Mandela's 65th birthday. He told an audience of 600 to fight against the fact that "the Caribbean Islands have been used more than once as half-way stations for shipping arms and war material, including nuclear warheads, from the United States and Canada to South Africa." In January 1983, Tambo led an ANC delegation to India and "called threatened Frontline States (Mozambique, Angola, Lesotho, Zimbabwe, Botswana, Zambia, Seychelles, Mauritius, Madagascar) against an undeclared war launched by the Pretoria regime." In February 1983, he was in Athens (capital of Greece) and Rome to receive, on behalf of Nelson Mandela, their awards of citizenship to Mandela. In the same year, the ANC had mobilized organs of the United Nations, the Organization of African Unity, 27 governments, 159 other governmental organizations and non-governmental organizations from Europe, Asia, North and South America, and the Caribbean to an "International Conference in Solidarity with the Frontline States." That conference "resolved to mobilize world opinion towards total isolation of the apartheid regime, and stopping the flow of support that sustains it." These would include oil embargos, an arms embargo, and bans on outside investments and loans to South Africa. By the late 1970s and early 1980s, the ANC had lit fires all over American University campuses and cities in calls for pulling investments ("disinvestment") out of South Africa. The world had began to recognize the ANC as the legitimate and alternative government in South Africa. This was a historic achievement by the ANC under the leadership of Oliver Tambo.

In 1976, the children of Soweto dropped a nuclear bomb on apartheid. It was a political nuclear bomb. Television hit the world with vivid pictures of their uprising against their inferior education, and the plot to cage them into a vast intellectual ghetto by replacing teaching them English, an international tool, with Afrikaans, a local linguistic hoe. The courage of the children against heavily armed and gun-firing white policemen, their mutual compassion for each other as symbolized by a boy of fourteen crying as he carried in his arms a fatally wounded schoolmate, also fell into the consciousness of television viewers and newspaper readers all around the world like a political nuclear bomb. Coming in the wake of the triumph of General Giap's Tet offensive in Vietnam and the humiliating flight of the American Ambassador and his staff out of Saigon, it sent deeper into world public consciousness that a profound "psychological disruption of the population" was occurring in North America, Western Europe, Asia, and South America among those who support racial oppression and exploitation of man by man.

Jimmy Carter came into the American presidency as a beneficiary of this condition. The Vietnam War had benefited those Americans who earned huge profits and dividends from the "military industrial complex." The Vietnam War had killed both President Johnson's promise of a better life for the poor in America (which included most of the American South), but also maimed and killed hundreds of thousand of their children. Jimmy Carter, the farmer of groundnuts or "peanuts," as the symbol of the smallman who had succeeded in becoming Governor of his State of Georgia, even walked to the White House after his swearing-in ceremony.

For the ANC, Jimmy Carter started making the right foreign policy noises. He appointed Andrew Young, an African-American, as Ambassador to the United Nations. Soon thereafter, the world was treated to the photojournalism drama of Andrew Young and David Owen, the British Foreign Secretary, stomping tarmacs in Pretoria and in Namibia, and blowing dust into the eyes of apartheid. But Carter did not last. He was blown out of office by a Reagan wind of conservatism and "constructive engagement" with South Africa.

Oliver Tambo's frustration and anger were naked: "The Reagan Administration," he told the Afro-Arab Conference on December 6-9, 1981, in Luanda, Angola's capital, "is going all-out to strengthen its relations with all reactionary forces that it can find among the Arab and African peoples...to ensure that the Afro-Arab zone is bisected by a string of military allies of the United States, stretching from Israel in the North, through the Arab world and the African continent, to South Africa in the South."[2] UNITA and RENAMO were Reagan's bandits, he said, to be used "to wipe out of existence the people's Republic of Angola...Mozambique,

Lesotho, Zimbabwe, and Zambia." Oliver Tambo's anger also had a military reason behind it.

The successes of the military units of the ANC had by the late 1970s already succeeded in causing a bitter split inside the South African ruling forces. The military officers were angry. A 1977 White Paper on Defense openly talked of "lack of coordinated national action." Vorster, the then President, was soon replaced by P.W. Botha, who had been the Minister of Defense from 1966 to 1980. The all-powerful image of the South African armed forces had been shattered in full view of the world by the combined armed forces of Cuba and Angola, with the logistic support of the Soviet Union. The official organ of the ANC, *Sechaba*, could write in its June 1983 issue that in the past decade, however, the balance of power had shifted significantly. "The initiative now lies firmly in the hands of the forces of liberation."

The pictures of a stampede of Americans and their Vietnamese allies scrambling to enter military helicopters on top of the American Embassy in Saigon; of hundreds of thousands of American students and the general public demonstrating against the war in Vietnam, Laos, and Cambodia; of FRELIMO, MPLA, and PAIGC forces and militants celebrating victories over Portuguese armed forces, and national liberation in Mozambique, Angola, and Guinea Bissau; of Soweto children in running battles with murderous South African armed forces, etc. were also sending into the Soviet Union, Poland, Rumania, East Germany, Bulgaria, and Czechoslovakia messages of Seme's "new and unique civilization."

In early December 1989, two senior executives of the Voice of America bought me lunch at the Space Center in Washington, D.C. One of them suddenly said: "Mikhail Gorbachev is a CIA agent." I retorted defensively by saying that he must have just finished reading a novel set in Tokyo in which the President of the Soviet Union was a CIA agent, as well as the one by the Australian former British intelligence agent who claimed that former British Prime Minister, Harold Wilson, was a Soviet spy. But, he looked decidedly triumphant. Whatever the truthfulness of that description of Gorbachev, he soon took momentous decisions under his policies of glasnost and perestroika. Soon he was toasting Reagan, and Reagan was toasting him at summits. Oliver Tambo suffered his first stroke. By 1990, the USSR had collapsed and disintegrated as a state. Communist parties, which won democratic elections according to Western multi-party dictates were driven out of Georgia and Khazakstan by armed groups backed by Western intelligence organizations.

In November 1989, I was invited with over three hundred other academics, to the Carter Center in Atlanta, Georgia. Other guests at the opening symposium pulled the audience to about eight hundred people. Professor Richard Joseph, an African-Caribbean-American, and a personal friend, was probably the one who got me on the list of those there. At the Carter Center, he was the "Professor of Democracy for Export to Africa." His real official title was much simpler than that. He was the "Master of Ceremonies," in Nigeria lingua. In introducing ex-president Carter, Richard Joseph (under the influence of the cultural drug he had consumed while at the University of Ibadan) announced Jimmy Carter "as the next President of the World." The audience gasped not too silently. Carter was compelled to rebuke Richard Joseph for being hyperbolic. Rakiya Omar, a young Somali woman with a beauty as sharp-edged as her brain and tongue, flew into a rage. She accused Carter of kissing cheeks with butchers like Siad Barre, Arap Moi, and Mobutu Sese Seko, etc. and yet claiming to be a "democrat," let alone nursing hopes of becoming a "world statesman."

There was something particularly striking about the Carter Center. There was a lot of Carter, or rather, of his hunger for a place in history. The walls in the corridors were all full of Carter in his days as President of the United States; of the past glory of the simple nuclear-scientist and "peanut farmer" from a backward South. Hunger is petrol inside human body; it drives it with a rare power. Perhaps, if Reagan had not derailed Carter's trajectory, he might well have fought an earlier end to apartheid, and saved Oliver Tambo from that debilitating stroke.

When Athens and Rome honored Mandela in February 1983, they did so for "The courageous example you set to your people and the entire world in the struggle for human rights against the oppressor, for the emancipation of your people." Honoring Nelson Mandela, the Commander-General in prison, was also, of course, giving honor to Oliver Tambo, the Commander-General who was outside South Africa. This is a status Jimmy Carter, as President, never had a chance to attain. This is a status, which perhaps Mikhail Gorbachev, as President of the Soviet Union, too might have longed to achieve. It is interesting that after his fall from power, Gorbachev called on Henry Kissinger, former American Secretary of State, to help him set up a "Gorbachev Foundation," for promoting "democracy."

In setting out to conquer the world by turning it against apartheid, Oliver Tambo, as leader of the ANC, served with utmost commitment and brilliant success, the fulfillment of Seme's promise that "The regeneration of Africa means that a new and unique civilization is soon to be added to the world."

Notes

1. *Sechaba*, "Unity in Action, Frontline States & Liberation Movements," (May 1983), pp. 29-31. See also *Sechaba*, June 1981; *Sechaba*, February 1982; *Sechaba*, March 1983; and *Sechaba*, June 1983.

14

ANY SDP/NRC PRESIDENTIAL SPEECHES TO MANGOES?

A billion-dollar saving through just one piece of agricultural research! That's an estimate of the worldwide economic value of a vaccine to protect poultry against Newcastle Disease. You are directly helped in many ways by agricultural research. The experiment stations had a big hand in developing today's meaty, tasty, economical chicken... In the first years after World War II, it took about four pounds of feed to grow one pound of chicken. Now, two pounds of feed make one pound of chicken. It used to take 14 to 18 weeks for poultry men to produce a chicken weighing four pounds. Today they raise a four-pounder in less than nine weeks....Potatoes are another productive miracle. Connecticut, where the first State Experiment Station started 100 years ago, grows as many bushels of potatoes now as in 1875, but this takes only a fourth as much land.

The words of Earl L. Butz, Secretary for Agriculture, United States of America, introducing *That We May Eat*, the 1975 Yearbook of Agriculture. But why go back to 1975? For two reasons. Earl Butz was the man who secretly sold so much wheat, maize, barley, and sorghum to the Soviet Union in the early 1970s that it caused a worldwide panic when poorer countries in South America, the Caribbean, Africa, Asia, and Europe woke up to find out that they had to scramble to buy less food at astronomical prices. Many American citizens turned to eating dog food and/or cat food because it was cheaper. When their prices also went up, the poor Americans turned to garbage bins as a food source. Throughout Africa, it forced governments to face the fact that colonial officials had always been feeding their officials (and growing urban populations) with food from foreign lands, having caused famines and established regimes of local food production as a permanent zone of poverty, as well as seclusion from rich European and American markets.

The other reason for going back to 1975 is that it was the 100th anniversary of the establishment of a Government Agricultural Research Station by the European immigrants to North America. One Paul Waggoner, the Director of the Connecticut station of New Haven (1975) said something worth repeating. He said with exuberance: "At the end of the first century of the Research Stations, we can point with pride at their accomplishments. Mostly, however, we see things to do. The Union of theory and practice in America's stations for discovery is a powerful force for improving the human condition. But, a century is only a beginning...."

Waggoner has startling news to back up his boasting. Agricultural scientists discovered vitamins. They discovered antibiotics such as *Streptomycin* and *Aureomycin*. Quinine, which came from a tree, was the antiballistic missile that saved European migrants to the tropics against certain death from malaria (the mosquito's submarine missiles). The first English settlers in North America faced a brutal and simple law: "Experiment and adapt, or die." In a single year (1609-1610), two-thirds of them in Jamestown, in the State of Virginia, had died. The wheat and barley seeds they had brought from England had produced nothing. Their host "Indians" came to their aid by giving them seeds of their own maize. The settlers planted them and buried heads of fish under the maize as fertilizer. It worked, and they had food to eat. But, they persisted with efforts to adapt their imported grain seeds. Heroes, like Samuel W. Johnson, who was propelled by "a desire to put science to work for society," started his mission in "a small laboratory at a family farm when he was eighteen years old." Legends are very vulnerable to spices invented by biographers, but there is something familiar in the story of a teenager cooking science in a family's rural kitchen. There is, in Africa today, an ignored tradition of colonial British, French, etc. doctors cooking surgery and other medical services inside grass-thatched huts, using oil lanterns and locally carpentered tables as platforms for their surgical operations. A reading of the *Daily Times* in the post-Civil War "money is not Nigeria's problem" era, however, shows a dense storm of the marketing invasion of Nigeria by Euro-American companies with the "most modern medical equipment found anywhere else in the world." If Nigerians didn't know how to spend oil money, these international companies were surely morally obliged to help! The colonial legacy of British doctors taxing their medical brains to not only diagnose diseases and perform surgical operations, but also invent equipment from local resources, was hurriedly and cynically buried by men and women who saw the marketing of medical technology as new frontiers for helping Nigerian leaders with the terrible dilemma of handling the new oil-money epidemic.

Americans export many things, including the "Ugly American"; and half truths about being a democracy. The city of Chicago, for example, uses the height of the Sears Company building, and the propaganda that an airplane takes off and lands in Chicago airport every half a second, etc., for glorifying itself. That propaganda does not, however, emphasize that it has one of the longest histories of brutal, corrupt, tribal, and racial terrorism in urban politics in the world. When Mayor Daley was in politics, an Irish ethnic mafia ran wards of the city of Chicago with combinations of bribery, vote-rigging, assassinations, etc. When Fred Hampton, a young Black Panther leader, set up centers where Black children were given breakfast as well as cultural pride and political education, both the Federal police boss, Edgar Hoover, and local politicians agreed that he must be assassinated. So he was gunned down as he slept in the depth of Chicago's political night.

But, there is grand American tradition of a popular culture of scientific invention, which they do not export. The multi-billion dollar *"peanut butter"* (pounded fried groundnuts) was invented by a Black man in a laboratory inside a rural hovel on a farm. Another Black man invented what makes blood not clot so that it can be kept for transfusion and transfer to another person. A young white boy was told by his doctor that he would die of cancer in less than three months. But, he got that news after it had occurred to him that the stone, which he had thrown into the air and which came down again, need not have come down. He could create a rocket, which would have a power greater than the dictatorial hands of the power of gravity. He swore to achieve that goal. That drive silenced the cancer in him. He lived to the age of seventy. In short, there is a dense forest of American folklore which says that American science has been and is the business, the product, the challenge, of every American no matter how young or how rural, how isolated he or she is. Science, popularly derived, has been the engine of American power. The real picture today is, of course, not that simple. Multinational companies are probably the biggest owners of scientists working in great secrecy to produce new wonder products. But they are not undermining that folklore and its potency.

When the East African Community was in terrible danger of collapse in 1971, all roads led to Nairobi, the Kenyan capital. Charles Njonjo, the Attorney General, and Bruce Mackenzie, the Minister of Agriculture, were allegedly the hatchet men who white settlers, the Americans, and the British were using to break up the Community. Njonjo had recently married the daughter of a Kenyan white settler. British and local white pilots wanted East African Airways broken up because Tanzania and Uganda had vigorously pursued the policy of training African pilots. The white pilots had been using the East African Airways as an arena for piling up flight hours, which would better their chances of getting employment with European airlines, etc. So we too ran to Nairobi to put up some fight. The Ugandan members of the Community's parliament were no problem. We urged them to target their Makerere College classmates in the Kenyan bureaucracy, especially those close to Kenyatta. We targeted community officials of the East African Posts and Telecommunications, the East African Railways and Ports Authority. To the Ugandans among them, we told them of the killings Amin's regime was secretly perpetrating on top officials both military and civilian. Then, we charged at the research scientists in meteorology, fisheries, animal research, etc. But, two walls kept banging our faces. Rivalries between Ugandan, Kenyan and Tanzanian officials in each area punctured needed solidarity and mutual closing of ranks. Then, their fear of politics. "We are not politicians. How can we confront Charles Njonjo and Mzee Kenyatta?" We chased after John Malecela, the executive secretary general of the Community, and caught up with him in a hotel where some Community parliamentarians were staying. He was desperate. We were angry. We accused him of failing to mobilize his agemates in all the three governments as well as the Community's officials to openly make statements in opposition to the unseen enemies of the Community. We were obviously being rash, insensitive, and unfair to Malecela.

I left Malecela and my companions, and took a walk into a park outside of the Kenyan Parliament. A car drove into the park to catch up with me. A "Socialist" British academic teaching at the University of Dar es Salaam and personally known to me was alone in the car. He was blunt. "What had John Malecela told you?" he demanded. I turned and kept walking with my silence. He was on duty, trailing his targets. I admitted to admiring the British technology of power. It hurt me so deeply that the research scientists of the East African Community, for example, were illiterate in that technology of politics and diplomacy. For with the collapse of the Community they would each return to small, poorly funded research institutes in their small wretched countries.

What is the moral of this story? While on a trip from Zaria to Abuja, we started complaining about the greed of Nigerian Mango trees. They remain green all year around. They flower only once a year and yield fruits, which take forever to ripen (if allowed to stay on that long). After that, they go into silence and indifference to our vitamin needs for a whole year. What kind of plant scientists would fight these mangoes, and force out of them more fruits more times a year? Why don't politicians go to these mangoes and harangue and promise them better schools so that they can become more productive?

A week later (May 25, 1993) *The Guardian* newspaper had just carried a story of a tribal meeting of research scientists. They said: "Its (government's) attendant insensitivity to matters affecting the nation's research capabilities, lipservice to science and technology has given rise to the near total lack of funding of research." It is tempting to contrast this scientific whimpering with how Hajiya Leila Dogonyaro and her army of women roared out a political summons, which had SDP's presidential candidate, Chief Abiola, rushing to Abuja to plead with them for forgiveness and to make juicy promises to the women. But that is another story. Or, is it really?

Earl Butz had been Dean of the Faculty of Agriculture at Purdue University when appointed President Nixon's Secretary of Agriculture. Purdue had created a political constituency over the years with the products of their agricultural researchers, which farmers, and especially huge multinationals, had turned into billions of dollars. He was not a man you could accuse of being handsome or charismatic. It was not his ethnic identity that got him the job. When he secretly sold billions of dollars of grain to the Russians in 1975, it was not to benefit his ethnic group, but to please "the American farmers." The lesson is clear. The African researcher has to turn his research product into a political irrigation spray sprinkler through open political campaigns among rural farmers by telling them how many billions of naira they would earn from the research findings they have already made, and would continue to make if only politicians and governments would act correctly. Only then would politicians at state and federal levels go out to make speeches to mangoes, mushrooms, cows, shrimps, and beans—and to agricultural research scientists. More importantly, only then would politicians, governments, and research scientists stop regarding scientific research as the monopoly of a rare few, who work in million-naira laboratories. A folklore of celebrating and honoring mass participation in scientific research (by roadside mechanics, rural gari processors, etc.) obviously deserves center stage in national politics all across Africa.[1]

Notes

1.   Frantz Fanon, *The Wretched of the Earth*, (London: Penquin, 1982) treats the disastrous historical impotence of African rulers in the challenge for the development of a post-colonial society from a non-racial context; seeing the problem rather as the product of inadequate de-traumatizing experiences resulting from not engaging in military combat against white colonial oppressors.

15

THE NEGLECTED HUMAN
TECHNOLOGY

"Your teeth are white and hard but they are weaker than milk. Has that entered your head? No one owns the poverty of not having cattle."

A riddle inside a rhetorical question (which was actually a deadly threat), which ended with a military law. Translated in brutal language, the military law went something like this: "If you can die in defense of the cattle you are herding in the wilderness, so can the other man who is trying to take them away from you." Whenever it was uttered, I always thought I noticed that the older women in the compound would let out sharp gasps, quicken the pace at which they were each doing whatever they were doing, and especially tell us where we could find our midday meal when we returned the cows for milking. As for me, I thought the burden of our father's ritual message was meant for my older brother to understand. My interest was in the fun of being out there throwing stones and sticks at birds, chasing squirrels, imagining myself owning the heroic task of surprising a sleeping antelope and catching both its hind legs as my brother rushed to spear it dead. Then there were the chasing, throwing sticks at, beating or shouting at the usual three or four cows and bulls in each herd who specialized in spying on you and—just as your alertness flagged—quickly taking swipes at heads of someone's crops. Like rain water, these ritual "anti-riot acts," which our father issued every morning whenever it was the turn of our home to look after the communal cattle herd, seeped into my mentality slowly, looking for roots to climb into.

There was also a ritual war game we played in teams. Each team provided a contestant armed with a flexible twig from a plant species whose bark, when pulled out, was full of a sticky wax. For this war game, the bark was not removed. The contestants hit each other as hard and as fast as possible. Whoever showed the expression of pain lost the contest. The next stick game was more dangerous, and reserved for the bigger boys. The sticks were barkless, dry, and hard to break. Every part of the body except the eyes was a target. The art of combat was in faking a direction of a hit and thus by passing the protective embargo of the opponents stick. Although the head could be hit, there was an informal code of war to avoid it for fear of drawing blood. The ultimate achievement was in catching hold of the opponent's stick, threatening to bash open his exposed head, heeding the chorus of appeals for mercy from all around, and merely hitting him once on the body and then running and jumping in triumph. The terror of losing was in the shame of the news when you came back home. It was a wise ploy (when such a disaster had happened to one) to bring the cows home and quickly slip away to spend the night in a relation's or a friend's home. *"Your teeth are white and hard but they are weaker than milk."*

School soon took me away. From primary seven, I entered the barracks life of successive missionary boarding schools. The first school admitted only eighty students after a competitive examination attended by candidates from more than twenty primary schools from five language-based colonial administrative districts. We were a polyglot of mother-tongue speakers who were compelled to speak only English at all times; spies were everywhere to report breakers of this law of one-language dictatorship. Every morning we rose to do physical drills which emphasized running on the same spot, stretching arms forward, above the head, away from the chest, and bending down to touch toes of both bare feet, etc. From four to six in the evening we played the game of chasing a round hard ball, colliding into each other, dribbling each other and kicking it into a net, past a goalkeeper who was the only one allowed to use his hands to hold, punch, or push away the ball during play. In primary eight a strange thing happened. The first African teacher arrived. He also not only played this game called "football" (while he was coaching us) but was also a player on the country's team. There was no talk of a "National Team" then. That terminology only crept in slowly after our country "became independent from British colonial rule." But our games at home with flexible and hard sticks were not in the school syllabus. No teacher told us every morning that law: *"Your teeth are white and hard but they are weaker than milk."* In fact, there were no cattle around. Instead of milk, we each received a spoonful of cod liver oil once a week. It smelled and tasted terrible.

Many years later, in a different ecology, my past as a cowherd exploded forth. It was along the road between the Tegina Junction and Kontagora town in northern Nigeria. The tarmac road ran alone, endlessly, through a vast savannah vegetation, like a river permanently under threat of being grown over by that silent vegetation. I was running back from borrowing a film on the construction of the TANZAM Railway linking Tanzania and Zambia. I wanted my students of public Administration to see the various policy innovations which the governments of China, Tanzania, and Zambia had woven into the construction of the railway line. I had first seen the film in the United States during the buildup to Nixon's historic visit to China. The Chinese Embassy officials in Lagos were most generous in lending it to me. Anyhow, at this spot in the savannah between Kontagora and the Tegina Junction, the skies were now blueblack with a threatening rain. There were no villages in sight. This herdsboy had talked his cows into forming a solid circle of a standstill solidarity. He himself was squatting under the biggest bull. "So far away from home," I said to myself. My father's military law came back too: *"Your teeth are white and hard but they are weaker than milk.... No one owns the poverty of not having cattle."* I was carrying a Chinese TANZAM Railway film on a long lonely road, which lay under permanent threat of being grown over by a vast savannah vegetation. Was it because I had once shared something in common with that herdsboy who was combating that vast savannah vegetation and an awesome sky by squatting under a bull?

Had my teachers used the game of football to make my education an act of betrayal, of rupture, of not developing new weapons for him and all herdsmen in Africa?

On Tuesday May 18, 1993, I stood watching primary school children at physical education in a school run by African Catholic nuns in a part of Abuja, Nigeria's new capital. Three main events were on. A female teacher blew a whistle in a rhythm. Her class, all very small girls, moved in a circle. Each girl twisted her waist and stamped the right foot against the ground according to the tune from out of the whistle. A nun in bluish-grey uniform struggled with a larger and older class. She was conducting an athletics team completion. Although the children were about the same body group, they wore four different uniforms. Four contestants (one each from the four uniform groups) lined up, set, and streaked off across a field to touch a tree at the end, and then ran back. The cheering teammates of winners charged forward to hug and hail their winning stars. The nun would, each time, be overwhelmed as finishing lines moved forward with the charging cheerers. No techniques were imparted. No technical lessons for those who lost. But the Mary Onyalis, Adenikans, Chidi Imos, and Carl Lewises were being born in naked rawness. Finally, the biggest group were matched out to military music with two military men in full uniform in attendance. It was a "match-past drill." The two male teachers who walked and ran about (as need dictated), were not as smartly dressed as the students and the soldiers were. "Times change," I thought to myself. But I remembered the herdsboy squatting under the biggest bull on the Tegina Junction to Kontagora Road, and wondered whether these physical education exercises were designed to produce those who will give him new technologies against that vast savannah and awesome skies.

The British teach cricket only to their ruling classes. A very hard ball is flung at you from a short distance with hidden techniques ranging from rib or skull-cracking speed, to fast but spinning balls, which assume unexpected trajectories on touching the ground, etc. Meanwhile, mean, hostile, fast-footed men with lightening reflexes crowd around the targeted enemy batsmen to "do him out." The language used is, of course, more gentle, like "caught out," "ran-out," "balled out," or "leg-before-wicketed."

There is a short and sharp celebration when the victim falls, while he, in turn walks away, head-up. No tears, no tantrums, no punches at his adversaries. Power is mean. You take your hits but keep your head up to fight another day. Grand successes like hitting a boundary for four or six runs at once is glory for the "batsman" but a terrible humiliation for the "baller." The British Empire was after all built with the broken bones of other peoples and races by British ruling classes bred through this human technology.

The Americans decolonized and republicanized the British game of rugby and made it more openly vicious. The British mess you up with slyness. They talk of plots for your murder with their teeth well protected against their cold snow—the "tight upper lip." The Americans wanted a more open show of power. So they renamed rugby "football" so that the players can use their feet and run to bash into each other like rhinos or buffaloes. The fastest men play on the wings. The oval ball is thrown at them from way back. Having taken off on speed when play started, they run and dodge at top speed to be at a particular spot to make a spectacular catch. The thrilling catches are by those who on grabbing the ball then proceed to outrun all their attackers and cross over a scoring line. The spectacular play is by one, who amid a dense forest of attackers, still makes a seemingly impossible catch just across the scoring line for the "touch down." That is the fun side of it; the side that makes one a hero on television screens across the vast country and brings in millions of dollars as a salary. The deadly side of it is when just as the great catcher is grabbing the fleeting ball, the opponent defensive player simultaneously hits him on the back, breaking his spinal cord. Many are called and many end up in wheel chairs with permanent paralysis. America is a land of vast fortunes, but just as it has wiped out millions of Native Americans, African slaves, European immigrants, it will also reward only the tough, ruthless "Superman." Super power comes with a human technology that breeds the "tough guy."

But what is the point of all this storytelling? It is to raise the question of human technology. The ancient cattle peoples of Africa, for example, invented human technologies for protecting the cow, the golden animal. The youth were trained in technologies of courage against the wilderness with its lions, leopards, hyenas, and human thieves. *You die that the cow may sustain the tribe.* If need be. The Japanese man used to cut off his little finger in front of his girlfriend and give it to her to keep as a sign of his devotion to her even though he was going away on a journey. An island country has the sea as friend, feeder, and graveyard. An island country which also knows very cold winters has two natural enemies. The mind and the heart, in such a country, are permanently under siege. You need a counter human technology for the survival of the race. Such traditional human technologies have been well recreated, cautiously adapted, and intelligently held onto, to meet the threat of the scientific European invader. I wonder whether that is perhaps why the ultimate Japanese hero, the wrestler, is so super-fat, like a human Nippon mountain: a super power even in a mortal flesh.

The story of the survival of the African man in the Americas is a vast library of human technologies for survival. The legendary late Alex Haley Wrote *Roots* as a new manifestation of this phenomenon. When he wrote *The Autobiography of Malcolm X*, with Malcom's cooperation, no one noticed then that he was engaging in an earlier version of this craft. A whole vast field lies out there for researchers to trace back which modes—Igbo, Hausa, Mandingo, Kong, Lunda, Wolof, Yoruba, etc.—of human technologies proved to be the most effective, the most indestructible, the most versatile for the survival of the African races in Peru, Brazil, North America, etc. We need them re-exported back. Above all, we need to focus on developing the African science of human technology so that we can link what children are being taught in schools and universities in each African country to the development of our survival tools in the twenty-first century. Nigeria has the human diversities to anchor this science.

The Reagan Administration openly showed its hostility to that ancient and time-tested African medical and social security system known as the "Extended Family Obligations and Duties Charter." His officials saw it as responsible for that post-colonial African concept of the new nation state as a collective polygamous family. African governance is exercise in the fulfilling of moral duties of the father, etc. This had given rise to mushrooming of government parastatals and corporations as tools for running African politics and national economies as collective household and community farming. Capitalism, said President Reagan, must smash down this social technology of the cobweb society through "privatization," "free trade," and government indifference to the health, feeding, housing, and laughters of its citizens. In short, the West (of which Reagan was the captain) was taking the issue of African human technology very seriously. African-Americans have a simple law. It goes like this: "If the white folks in America do not like something which the Black folks are doing, then there must be something very good in it for Black folks, which they should fight to keep and promote."

But there are problems too. Two examples can illustrate some of them. The British Government organized the overthrow of the Obote Government in Uganda in 1971 because he was telling the British to take away those Asians in Uganda who were British citizens. Why? Because they monopolized import, export, and retail trade, thanks to colonial laws which had prohibited Africans from owning shops within a distance of ten miles from a "trading center" or urban area. The Asian traders also fixed prices by fiat. They sat in secret community meetings and fixed prices of commodities arbitrarily. If government increased salaries of civil servants today, tomorrow the Asians would increase prices. The African civil servants began to see themselves as working and sweating for the Asian traders. Disenchantment built up into creeping racial hostilities. Obote started talking to the British. The Asians became more nervous, and in anticipation of deportations, began to intensify the use of over invoicing, making sure that every Asian child of twelve imported a brand new car as a way of sending money out, etc. They were into massive disinvestment from the Ugandan economy. Unemployment went up. Obote fell. Then Amin came down with his anti-Asian thunder. "Leave with immediate effect," he roared, and it worked.

In Nigeria, there are clans that control areas of trade and economic activities. Like the Asian in Uganda, they meet and fix prices. If their "son of the soil" is the boss of the distributive sector of a public company, the clan moves in to monopolize "distributorship" nationwide. On June 1, 1993 I heard an angry friend ask a lawyer why there are no laws in Nigeria against monopolies and collusion to fix prices. Why does the government wait until public frustration at such ethnic monopolies and price fixings has exploded into periodic communal violence and mayhem to make noises, which do not address the basic cancer? The lawyer sounded evasive in his response. He knew of cases, he said, where traders who control a particular line of business will arrange "to have you killed if you try to enter and offer competition."

He had dodged the big legal question, and rebuke. In short, the need for human technology and the rise and fall of the demons of Bosnianization, Somalianization, and Liberianization of Nigeria is an urgent one. It deserves creative and not merely destructive or demolition intervention.

We can end this glimpse from under the thickets of fantasyland. How about the Organization of African Unity (OAU) running an annual program of each of the 54 Heads of State in Africa hosting two youths (one boy, one girl, making a tiny total of 108 youths) drawn from each African country as their African extended family relations, for one month? The OAU Secretary General can be the "contractor" to run the project, with my consultancy fees built in as my donation to the new African Extended Family.

16

TRUSTING JAMAICA MAN

The visit to Nigeria by the Prime Minister of Jamaica, P. J. Patterson (popularly referred to as "PJ" when he was Foreign Minister in Michael Manley's government in the mid 1970s when I visited that island country), is a good enough reason to gossip about the Caribbean and its African character. PJ's term of office as Foreign Minister in that period came together with an important tilt towards Africa in Jamaican politics and popular culture.[1] The Prime Minister, Michael Manley, a "very *brown man*" (the local terminology for a very light-skinned man whose mother was a white woman), had suddenly betrayed his ethnic group, the middle-class (Jamaica's code name for the light-skinned class) by marrying a dark-skinned beauty. She, in turn, started a radio program in which she told her weekly audiences African folk tales and their hidden meanings for social behavior. This was touching on an ancient rural Jamaican legacy of grandmothers telling their ninies, Anansi spiders tales by moonlight. Anansi is a Ghanaian word, and such tales also reminded people of one Akampong (ancient relation of today's Acheampongs) who led an undefeated guerrilla warfare struggle for freedom against British troops for liberation from slave work. To this day, he is a national hero in Jamaica.

This development came simultaneously with a flurry of invitations to presidents Kenneth Kaunda, Mwalimu Nyerere, Samora Machel and others. They came bringing with them the flavor of revolutions and liberation struggles by *Black* African peoples against *white* domination. In Jamaica, the conservative but highly respected newspaper, *The Daily Gleaner,* openly articulated its sympathy with the white racists in Rhodesia and South Africa. The paper's impact was vividly illustrated for me by a Black youth who came up to me at a "middleclass" party (where Mozart and not Bob Marley was being danced to) and started lecturing me about how everything had collapsed in Haiti ever since three hundred years ago when Black people took away power from white people. It was only after his lecture and praises of the better wisdom of Jamaicans in matters of who should hold political power, that he asked me when I had left my country Haiti and fled to Jamaica.

In contrast to that youth, Bob Marley and the Wailers picked up the theme of liberation at home and identification with liberation struggles in Africa.

A calypso song I had liked before visiting Jamaica had this lyric: *"Never, never trust a Jamaica Man... He is the dread of the Caribbean."* What could it mean, I asked. Then I saw a play in a theater in Mona suburb. A school girl and a school boy who rode the same bus back home each day felt a special pull towards each other. Each subconsciously saw a feature of their father in the other. Papa was sowing seeds in many fields, working under the silence. It turned out that historically the lack of land and abundance of poverty had driven Jamaican men to migrate to Panama to construct the Panama Canal; leave for Cuba to cut sugar cane; to do work which the British poorer classes no longer agreed to do and run to New York and Canada. The women were poorly left behind. Too many for the fewer men. So each man had to cultivate so many other fields if there were to be social peace and mental health all around. The women, however, held the fabric of society together, drawing from African traditions of the power grandmothers and the extended family system—or whatever remained of it.

And quite a lot of Africa had remained. I first made contact with goat pepper soup in Kingston. At every social party (or fette), goat pepper soup was served exactly when the clock hit midnight. The music stopped. Dancing stopped. The blessing of the goat was followed by rice-and-beans. Tradition had to be obeyed by the middle classes too. Then there were the market women—the Higglers, as they are called. They controlled the food from the villages sold in town. And in the market they sat with thighs wide apart, both arms resting on a bridge of a tucked-in rappa. I had first seen it in Accra, Ghana. I was to see it again outside the central market in Georgetown, Guyana. The Manley government was making these traditions respectable for the first time.

Driving on a road which climbed up into the "mountain" ridges which run from east to west in central Jamaica, I stopped in at a rural school to watch a football match between a local and a visiting school team. The children could have come from Tafawa Balewa in Bauchi State in Nigeria, from Kisangani in eastern Zaire, or from outside Tries in Senegal. Same hair, some variation in tones of African skin color, and same skinny legs from malnutrition. They had will and intense school nationalisms driving them, but their bodies lacked power. They were severely undernourished. Coming to the school I had borne witness to little huts perched on hillsides with small patches of food crops being grown on soils in between rock boulders. The radio had often carried reports of houses in the rural hills being washed away by heavy rains. Driving away from the school football drama I saw a vast field of sugar cane. It was (I was told by my guide) owned by a British family with long roots in the history of Jamaica. Jamaica grows sugar cane and bananas on its best lowlands to sell abroad to earn foreign exchange. The villager struggles to sustain his race and class on patches of land hanging dangerously from hillsides. Caribbean food and nutrition conferences held in Kingston, and several weeks later in Barbados confirmed that the scenario in Jamaica was typical of the whole region. And, in each island (St. Lucia, St. Thomas, St. Kitts, Trinidad and Tobago, Barbados, etc.), it was the dark-skinned majority who also dominated landlessness and desperate poverty. The rumblings on the university campus in Kingston (from which Walter Rodney had been prevented from further teaching in 1968), were assuming louder and louder tones of "Black Power." Walter Rodney, the famous Guyanese historian, had been declared a security risk by the Jamaican ruling classes when he started telling large open air classes in the poorest areas in Kingston that their ancestors had built the Oyo Empire, the Benin Empire, the Songhai and Mali empires, and a university in Timbuktu. The myth that Black peoples had no civilization was a racist myth. He taught and preached a new consciousness. By the mid 1970s, P.J. Patterson was inviting African presidents and revolutionaries to address mass rallies in Jamaica. Rodney had made his work.

Before leaving for Barbados, a Jamaican friend told me that all male persons who are visiting Barbados are warned never to bend down to pick a coin which has fallen from their hands. "It is a terrible health hazard. It is an invitation to an instant rape." The joke hits at a legacy of homosexuality, which upper-class English folk exported with their migration to that small island. One leaves Bridgetown, the capital, in the morning and, with picnic stops on their wonderful beaches, returns in the evening, having driven all around Barbados. That is how small it is. The story is also told that Bajans (the people of Barbados) went into a terrible national panic when former Nigerian President General Gowon arrived there. As soon as Gowon's huge entourage had spread out at the airport tarmac, the permanent winds that cool the tropical island went still. Silent. The luxurious *babanrigas* (gowns) of Gowon's delegation had, in their billows, eaten up all the host nation's winds.

Both jokes are typical Jamaican jokes. They mocked the social as well as the industrial backwardness of the smaller islands in the Eastern Caribbean. Barbados needs the winds to attract tourists to its tropical beaches. *Wind is the poor nation's only industry.* The Jamaicans also had for a long time hosted the only university for the region. By the early 1970s, Guyana started one by themselves, amid derisive insults from the arrogant Jamaicans, especially their Oxford, Cambridge, and London School of Economics alumni.

But why tell all these ancient tales? Because it would appear that Nigeria's foreign policy commitments to defending and promoting the interests and dignities of the Black man everywhere, is not reflected much in the local media's coverage of these peoples and their countries. Because of this media silence, there is little, if any, public contribution to policies towards these people. They are the invisible brothers. Until the Seoul Olympics, neither the

Nigerian nor African media in general had written about a Jamaican-born Johnson, "The Bullet." The public knows not what impact a university in Jamaica built by Nigeria or the OAU would have on developments in the region. (The admissions exercise for it would presumably be beyond the reach of the Joint Admissions and Matriculation Board).

Someone made a nasty joke recently that the late Prime Minister of Guyana had set Walter Rodney ablaze because he mistook his crouched body for a pig owned by a Guyanese Indian. The Prime Minister's name was Forbes Burnham. It is a sick joke whose underlying political pathos and tragedy the African media are not helping to elucidate for their audiences across the continent.

A 1992 BBC report on Blacks in Colombia, South America, carried voices of peoples of African descent who had a very advanced idea of how they got there. Their ancestors, one said, had sailed across the Atlantic Ocean just like Christopher Columbus had done later, following them. This is a theory, which professor Van Sertima, an African-American historian has developed into a pathbreaking book, *They Came Before Columbus.* Does the current reparations campaign include these African-Americans too? The public in Africa cannot be expected to debate such issues if the press continues to organize silence about the African Diaspora. Or be warned against trusting a Jamaica Man.

Notes

1. *Time,* April 12, 1993, p.19, claimed that the March 20, 1993 elections in Jamaica "turned less on issues than on personalities," while the BBC stated that the *racial pride* of the majority Black electorate was the deciding factor, since P.J. Patterson, the incumbent Prime Minister is Black—the first ever to rule Jamaica. His People's National Party won 53 out of 60 seats.

17

DID DR. MARTIN LUTHER KING, JR. KILL PRESIDENT JOHN F. KENNEDY?

The questions of the three Ks—"Did King Kill Kennedy?" and "Did Kennedy Kill King?"—are at once outrageous, bizarre, and arresting. They are also cheeky, especially to official history, which cringes at such elevation of the Black masses of the United States into perpetrators of such grand criminality as causing the death of a heroic President or lowering the status of Kennedy into that of a desperate villain and an assassin of a Black "founding father."

It is obviously outrageous to even hint that Dr. Martin Luther King, Jr. could have *killed* anybody at all. He was a devotee of Mahatma Ghandi's philosophy of *nonviolence* as a means of undertaking the historical responsibility of fighting for freedom and rehumanizing a cruel society. In the face of an actual physical attack on him inside a church by a white member of the American Nazi Party; the bombing of four Black children in a church in

Birmingham, Alabama; beatings, breaking of legs, shootings by Alabama State Troopers under the direction of racist Governor Wallace, etc., King preached and practiced adherence to nonviolence built on unblinking love of the "enemy."

As for Kennedy, he owed King a special debt. His narrow victory over Richard Nixon in 1960 was traced to the African-American voters who voted overwhelmingly for him when word spread among them that Kennedy had personally telephoned King's anxious pregnant wife, Corretta, when her husband was thrown into jail on cooked-up charges and there were fears that he might be murdered by racist police and prison guards. He promised her help, and he got King out of jail. By 1963, just a year before the next Presidential elections, King had amassed a 500,000 (by the most liberal estimates) *multi-racial* "March on Washington" rally, which was televised live throughout the country and rocked the nation with his instantly famous "I Have a Dream" speech, that "from every mountainside, let freedom ring. And if America is to be a great nation, this must become true. And when *this* happens...we will be able to speed up that day when *all* God's children, black men and white men, Jews and Gentiles, Protestants and Catholics, will be able to join hands and sing in the words of the old Negro spiritual, 'Free at last! Free at last! Thank God Almighty, we are free at last!'" The politician in Kennedy made him greet King with the refrain "I have a dream" when the multiracial leaders of the rally called on him in the White House immediately after it had ended. That was a politician's salute in search of votes. It could not have been a code word for King's assassination.

But the four-word questions will not be silenced that easily when one swims and floats through a tapestry of history and memory recaptured by Taylor Branch in his 922-page narrative, *Parting the Waters.*[1] It is about a galaxy of stars of sacrifice, daring, mental and physical animation, emotional ignition and conflagration; of bullets of consciousness spurted out by rupturings of preachers and radio newscasters; television and newspaper broadcasts of horrendous, chilling, enraging, or enchanting pictures of human actions. The human actors and stars range from wretchedly poor and illiterate Black sharecroppers trapped in rural Mississippi; to rabid white haters of Black folk in the Alabama police force; to an introverted Black folk in the Alabama police force; to introverted Black law student at Yale University who suspends his own schooling to go and undertake that most dangerous task of encouraging frightened rural Black poor to dare to go to a racist white registrar and utter those most hazardous words, "I want to register to vote"; to cowardly African-American rich and educated classes; to clandestine spooks and investigators from the Federal Bureau of Investigation (FBI) planting telephone-tapping devices for overhearing King's sexual exploits; to President Kennedy and his staff; to king and his political team; to courageous school children in Birmingham being bitten by police dogs, battered with police water-jets, and crammed into jails. Sadistic white Alabama prison guards in fits of political rage tear out the eye of a young Black woman; shatter the teeth of a white male student Freedom Rider, and an assassin blows a hole from the back through the body of Medgar Evers (a Black activist who assists and encourages Blacks to struggle to get registered as voters) as he reaches the door of his house. Federal government lawyers do mental tip-toeing through laws and court precedents in desperate attempts to blunt brutal and vicious uses of the courts by white segregationists against King and his army of utterly vulnerable demonstrators; Black college students walk into toilets "for whites only" in bus stations or sit at counters "for whites only" in restaurants, bus stations, and shops, and accept brutal beatings by irate white segregationists; and singing luminaries like Mahalia Jackson, Aretha Franklin, and Joan Baez use songs as weapons of combat at rallies for civil rights causes, etc. In short, history is not the stride of omniscient, omnipotent, god-like single individuals such as King and Kennedy.[2]

They are a part—significant, but only a part—of a galaxy of often simultaneous illuminations of individuals across vast expanses of distance, literacy, age, courage, vision, selfishness, and selflessness. In fact, neither King nor Kennedy were ever in control of this galaxy once it went into motion; often they gasped, felt faint, and struggled to keep afloat in streams of events ignited by others. It was indeed school children in Birmingham (many as young as six-years-old), who gave King their hearts, wills, and daring as the ladder with which to climb (from within a jail cell) to the mountaintop of social protest and challenge. It was the horrendous sights of seven-year-olds being bashed by police waterhoses, bitten by police dogs, having their legs jumped on and crushed by hate-filled white vigilantes, as captured by in newspapers and television cameras, which sent revulsions as well as rare inspiration across the nation and gave King a true political tallness. The children made King a force, while violently shoving Kennedy into the deadly political jungle of sending a Civil Rights Bill to Congress for passage into law, a mere one year before the looming 1964 elections. It must be said that it is the children who helped King in pushing Kennedy towards his physical death.

And yet, that is only part of the movement of the galaxy. There was a deadly man called Edgar Hoover, the boss of the FBI, one of the keepers of the secrets of the land, secrets of the brain of power. Hoover commanded a nationwide human and technological army for collecting information and turning it into deadly political weapons. His fatal touch came when he could prove that an American citizen or movement was a willful agent, puppet, or unknowing ally of the Kremlin and Soviet Communism.

Sensing King's historical trajectory quite early, he informed the Kennedy Administration that King had two men, one white (Levison) and one Black (O'Dell), who were agents of Russia. The "Negro Movement" led by King was (whether King knew it or not) therefore a Communist weapon for destroying the United States. When later on King's "March on Washington" revealed that a new power of awakened multiracial conscience was rocking the American condition, Hoover turned urgently brutal. In Taylor's words: "Hoover did not welcome a giant march for freedom by a race he had known over a long lifetime as maids, chauffeurs, and criminal suspects, led by a preacher he loathed." The other unspoken side of this terrible "Communist Negro Movement" was President Kennedy, its ally; the man it voted into office in 1960. Hoover instructed his men to insert his news reports about King's Soviet connections in newspapers in the South, including one in King's hometown *The Atlanta Constitution.* Southern white segregationists in and out of power and in congress got Hoover's message. The Civil Rights Movement was a Communist invasion from the Kremlin. Kennedy was a national security risk since he was a "nigger-lover."

Hoover also liked to skin his prey from all four legs. He alarmed the Kennedy team indirectly by attacking Vice-President Lyndon B. Johnson's personal assistant. The assistant, Bobby Baker, was in the business of obtaining lucrative rewards by securing girls for high government officials. One such girl, Ellen Rometsch, had arrived from East Germany five years earlier and was having an affair with President Kennedy. A newspaper in faraway Iowa, carried a tantalizing report that Rometsch, who was classed "as stunning and in general appearance comparable to movie actress Elizabeth Taylor," had just been quietly deported by the Justice Department, headed by Bobby Kennedy, the President's brother. Hoover also circulated his report on Bobby Baker's girls-trade to Senate leaders, and those from bugging King's conversation, as well as those of Levison, to the CIA, the Defense Department, and the State Department. Hoover's defense of racism in America was done with white segregationist guns and bombs blasting down "Negro churches," Black children, and voter registration workers, as well as with Hoover's intelligence missiles targeted at the Soviet Union, via a Kennedy body. Perhaps in this sense, King killed Kennedy with Hoover's wrath.

President Kennedy had earlier in 1963 led King outside of his office into the Rose Garden to whisper to him of the grave danger to the civil rights cause if the FBI leaked out information that some of his friends had communist stains. "If they shoot *you* down, they'll shoot us down, too," he warned. King apparently failed to return Kennedy's verbal generosity by warning him that if the racists in Alabama, Mississippi, Tennessee, etc. who had already been blasting down African-Americans in series of assassinations, went unpunished and unchecked by federal arms, soon they would assassinate him (Kennedy), too. Perhaps in this fatal reticence he killed Kennedy passively, with his silence, and actively, with the taste for blood which his movement had aroused among white segregationists nationwide, but more immediately in the South. Raw primitive passions oozed out of white officials and ordinary persons, as exemplified thus: "We killed two-month old Indian babies to take this country; and now they want us to give it away to the niggers."

Soon after the March on Washington, the philosopher Reinhold Niebuhr said on a television discussion with writer James Baldwin, that "all through history, it was a despised minority—the proletarian, the peasant, the poor—who recaptured the heights and depths of faith." He failed to give special note to the historic intervention of Black primary and secondary school children. College students pushed King from the pulpit into sit-ins; picket lines in front of segregating shops, hotels, etc., into the tedium and violence of voter registration. They pulled and dragged him into the drama of their youthful impulsiveness, determination, and imagination. Taylor's message is clear: a nation that cannot irrigate its arid present with the imagination, anger, and enthusiasm of its most poor and downtrodden—its children, its youth both in and out of college—is doomed to wallow in the "sin of triviality." This is a message which, in the current American context, so aptly and urgently awaits Bill Clinton as he faces the results of past "scorched earth" invasions by the Reagan-Bush Administrations (both at home and abroad) of ghettoes in Harlem, Chicago, Los Angeles, Washington, D.C., etc., with drugs, unemployment, and official deportations of millions of Americans from full citizenship into deadened marginality. Africa's case is on an even larger and more tragic scale, as the two American regimes sent over World Bank and IMF goons for bashing picnics of looting.[3]

The other lesson is the obvious one of whose historian is writing whose history. The assassination of President Kennedy in Dallas, Texas, was immediately written as a white technological event. Lee Harvey Oswald had shot a gun from a window. Oswald had mental problems. Oswald was quickly shot in the full glare of television cameras by another white man who hated communists, etc. The Warren Commission probably covered up the hidden hands of other, powerful white men. In this way, the historical quakes with which the African-American struggle for freedom had rocked the lives, passions, and visions of *all* Americans in gargantuan private and public spectacles, was immediately ignored.

It would not be allowed to have the historical and philosophical dignity of having forced change upon a nation: of holding national responsibility in its collective bosom. The lesson is clear: Have your own gazers upon the world, your own rakers of the sands of human actions. African foreign policy makers in the African Diaspora must invest in their own scholarship for global responsibilities. For how else would we know whether the questions "Did King kill Kennedy?" and "Did Kennedy kill King?" are not identical boobytraps.

Notes

1. Taylor Branch, *Parting the Waters: America in the King Years, 1954-1963,* (New York: Simon & Schuster, 1988) has the merit of combining giving information with the dramatic pulse of a Black pulpit preacher.

2. Six-part PBS documentary, *Eyes on the Prize* (1992), is a most touching complement to Taylor Branch's narrative.

3. Minion K.C. Morrison, *Black Political Mobilization* (New York: State University of New York Press, 1987) is a most valuable source.

18

NEW FLOWERS FOR CUBAN-AMERICAN RELATIONS[1]

"I want to be the first President of the United States to set foot on a free and democratic Cuba." So resonated a desperate but combative presidential candidate George Bush at a rally in Florida where about one million Cuban immigrants now live. He lost the election. Ironically, another Republican Party presidential candidate, Richard Nixon (then an incumbent Vice-President to President Eisenhower), had been forced in 1960 to deny the existence of a secret CIA plan, which he had already set in motion, to invade Cuba. Nixon called his rival an irresponsible warmonger for suggesting a United States military invasion of Cuba. Nixon's opponent was a younger Senator John F. Kennedy, who as a Roman Catholic, was seen as a sure loser in an America whose power elite had always been white Anglo-Saxon Protestants (WASPs). Kennedy won. Narrowly, but he won. Bill Clinton, who openly modeled his younger physical appearance and political thrust to that of Kennedy, was President Bush's opponent. All "natural" contenders in Clinton's Democratic Party had refused to run because they were sure that Bush would surely win. Clinton gambled and won. Overwhelmingly in electoral college votes, narrowly in votes cast, but he won. Less than ten weeks to stepping out of power, President Bush suffered a humiliating diplomatic defeat at the United Nations General Assembly when only three countries (including the United States and Israel) voted for the widening and continuation of American economic blockade of Cuba. Seventy-one countries abstained in the voting, including Canada (a fellow member of the new U.S.-Mexico-Canada common market). President Bush had, in the run to the Presidential elections, announced that all subsidiaries of U.S. multinational corporations based in other countries would be breaking American law if they continued to trade with Cuba, and foreign-owned ships which carried Cuban exports would be denied access to American ports.

The vote in the UN General Assembly had both gotten out of the way the putrid diplomatic Cold War garbage left behind by President Bush, and sent a clear message to Clinton that the rest of the world is tired of the stench of old bile in American attitudes towards Cuba. It is worth going over who should be tired. For a start, officials of the World Health Organization (WHO) and the United Nations Educational, Social, and Scientific Organization (UNESCO) have, since the early 1970s, been trumpeting their elation over Cuba's eradication of diseases such as polio, measles, malaria, malnutrition, and tuberculosis, as well as adult illiteracy among all her citizens, and achieving free and compulsory education up to university level for all. These are the scourges (some would callously say the "badges") of the Third Class World, the South. Cuba, a developing country, with an economy and geographical size far smaller than that of India, Indonesia, Brazil, Argentina, Nigeria, Egypt, and South Africa, has shown the world that these dreadful scourges are not a permanent birthright. The success of Cuba in rehumanizing her society and giving her people new horizons of individual and collective self-respect made the poverty, malnutrition, illiteracy, and high rates of homicide and violence among the poorer classes in the enormously rich United States seem even more disgraceful and indefensible. American leaders had no answer to an African-American political leader who, on visiting Cuba, said "If they are the evil things that communism brings, then I want some communism too." Cuba became UNESCO's and WHO's weapon for rebuking others, both rich and poor.

The Cubans also pioneered some very exciting educational ideas. They, for example, built new boarding secondary schools in which students combined academic learning with the management of full-fledged commercial agricultural projects whose products the students exported to urban consumers. Academic learning and productive practice were shown to be very beneficial and complementary. The student was no longer a dormant talent during all the years of academic learning. The Cubans also experimented with new techniques of student assessments and allocation of grades. Instead of examinations being rituals written in silence, in selfish secrecy and antagonistic survival-of-the-fittest situations, the students took part in assessing each other's verbal skills, leadership abilities, and show of caring for the welfare and interests of others, as exhibited by each one of them throughout the academic session. At the end of the session the class got together and awarded each other grades during open discussions. A final example was the educational use of stories and photographs in old newspapers which were in existence before 1961 (the year of the revolution) as teaching tools in primary and secondary school lessons. The idea was to show the children the terrible situations under which Cubans had lived in the past and what differences Castro's rule had brought. If they were to defend Cuba today they should know why it would be beneficial to do so.

For those from Vietnam, Nicaragua, Colombia, Bolivia, Angola, Mozambique, Algeria, Ethiopia, Jamaica, Guyana, etc., Cuba gave diplomacy a new human resonance. Castro's regime produced thousands of medical doctors, for example, for export to rural areas of these countries. In most countries, including the United States and Britain, rural communities find it very difficult to recruit and retain doctors for their clinics. The big money is in the big cities and not in rural hamlets. The golf courses and high society social events are also in or around the cities. Cuba supplied politically as well as medically trained doctors who knew the needs of rural peoples. The last time professor Ransome Kuti wanted them in Nigeria, the Nigerian Medical Association members almost hanged him with a thousand stethoscopes. In places like Jamaica and Grenada, the Cubans laced their manpower exports with Black Power pins. At a construction site for a Technical College just outside of Kingston, Jamaica, the racially mixed Cuban construction team was headed by a Black man! An undergraduate student who was our guide found this a very significant lesson for people in Jamaica.

African diplomats from Algeria, Mozambique, Angola, Namibia, Guinea Bissau, and Cape Verde (whose people had bled for long, gruesome years to win freedom) found in the Cubans a unique intellectual diplomacy for combat. The Cubans used their Institute for the Study of the Americans, for example, to collect data and write position papers, which guided their diplomatic activities at the United Nations and the Non-Aligned Movement. They were the first to circulate to African, Asian, and Latin American leaders their calculations about the new Debt War which began to blaze in the mid-1970s. Their calculations showed that the debts were rising in geometrical progression (by leaps and bounds). They were *not payable*. Solutions? *Refuse to pay them*. But, the point is that Cuba has bequeathed to Third World diplomats a legacy of academic research and permanent intellectual warfare. Diplomacy was for them not a matter of sleeping through United Nation debates deep in the embraces of alcohol. A nation may be small, yet accurate but embarrassing information is often a deadly tank in her armory.

For those in Africa who have had to shape public policies towards the African Diaspora, Cuba has been a virtual Mecca. From an African-Cuban population whose major industries in 1960 were prostitution, pimping, and being domestic servants, Castro had by the 1970s produced an Olympic champion, Theophelus Stevenson, who would refuse to fight for money, because (as he put it) the honor of fighting for his country could not be measured in millions of dollars. It was so much higher, a matter of his and his people's national dignity. Rural Blacks in Cuba, before 1960, were either poor, small farmers, housed in shacks, or workers on sugar cane plantations owned by American companies. The pay was very low, and most of them starved in the months when there was no planting and cutting cane to be done. They were illiterate, diseased, and malnourished. Castro's policies brought to them ownership of good flats and other housing units, free health care, free education for their children up to the highest levels, and full membership in the political drama of their country. By the time South Africa invaded Angola, the president of their country would say with pride that "African blood runs in the veins of every Cuban." And then, he sent them to fight for the freedom of African people in Angola as a matter of fulfilling their "international obligation." When they met other Black people in the Americas—from Peru, Colombia, Brazil, Mexico, Surinam, Panama, USA, etc.—they saw the visible difference between their own new confidence and bounce, as well as their freedom to aspire to the highest achievements in their country.

Of course, the Cubans have made many elsewhere chuckle at their tugging on the tail of the "American Lion" only ninety miles to their north. It has, for example, been part of their "revolutionary duty" to do cheeky things like beating the United States Basketball team at the Pan American games held in Cuba. The Yankees lost at the game their national genius invented on enemy territory, in front of an irate Cuban crowd. Then, at the 1992 Barcelona Olympic Games, not only did Castro go there in person to claim his roots, but the Cuban "*twits*" (to use angry Americanese) trounced the Americans in baseball (another American invention and, please note, an adaptation of cricket). These cheeky Cubans will stop at nothing to wage diplomatic war against a bully. But their adversary cannot deny their cultural Americanness when it comes to sports. Such a silly paradox.

It is fitting (those responsible for African policy towards the African Diaspora would say) that when Cuba hosted the World Athletics Championships, it was Africa that won it, with the Americas losing even second place to Europe. Cuba's record, in her recent humane treatment of Africa's children abroad, endears her most to Africa, and that record was fittingly honored by Africa's best athletes being the world's best on Cuban soil.

In these times when Cuban-American relations are at a critical crossroads, with the exit of a Cold War warrior and the entry of a "new age" warrior for the creation of the new humane American citizen both at home and abroad, African leaders must take the initiative pleading for a truce, a thaw, and a new exchange of flowers in Cuban-American relations. It will be a plea from a position of profound responsibility by African leaders and people to two of her blood relations who are still fighting a cold war whose embers died as Gorbachev's laughter tangoed with Reagan's.

Notes

1. The *Granma Weekly* (1978-1987) has been the major source of information on events in Cuba. It is ironical that a conservative philosopher like Ortega y Gasset may well have written these words regarding the political leadership of Cuba under Fidel Castro:

   > Really to live is to be directed towards something, to progress towards a goal....The apparent egoism of great men is the inevitable sternness with which anyone who has life fixed on some undertaking must bear himself.

19

AFRICA, THE YANKEES, AND THE AYATOLLAHS

"If a free society cannot help the many who are poor, it cannot save the few who are rich....In the long history of the world, only a few generations have been granted the role of defending freedom in its hour of maximum danger." That was the rhetorical flare of John F. Kennedy on his inauguration day as the new President of the United States. A visibly younger man in body and in mental energy, he carried with him the Cold War stings of the Eisenhower years together with new visions of Pax Americana as well as his promise of the United States landing a man on the moon "before this decade [of the sixties] is out!"

Many who listened to his address, including African-Americans, were convinced that they had heard firm promises for the betterment of their domestic oppression. After all, as Kennedy flashed his charisma across the nation, African-American students across the Deep South (in states like Tennessee, Mississippi,

Alabama, Arkansas, etc.) were involved in dangerous but politically electrifying dramas of sitting in restaurants, cinema theaters, and supermarkets from which racial discrimination had previously barred them. Kennedy's victory over Richard Nixon had (analysts had just discovered) been because of African-American voters giving him their votes. These hopes were to remain, in the main illusions. Eight days after that inaugural speech, Kennedy took over from Richard Nixon the secret planning of the invasion of Cuba and overthrow of Fidel Castro. Castro was a personal competitor with Kennedy for the smiles of the beautiful women of the Americas. He had a grand beard, a rare daredevil will, and an open program for curing the poverty of the oppressed. Another such competitor was out there in the jungles of the Congo (later Zaire)—one Patrice Lumumba. Finally, there was Nikita Kruschev at the Kremlin with that devastatingly frank-talking wit of his peasant Russian parents. Kruschev had just told the British that in Russian Cold War strategy, they were not a country, but a floating warship which would be sunk in thirty seconds.

Three months later, Castro humiliated Kennedy by defeating the Bay of Pigs invasion and capturing over one thousand American troops. Kennedy, however, bounced back by having Lumumba kidnapped and assassinated. Then, he blockaded Cuba and frightened the world with eyeball-to-eyeball nuclear brinkmanship with Krushchev. The Russian blinked first, and American *Macho* was rekindled and personified in Kennedy. His focus on foreign policy as the arena for the drama of grandeur both nationally and personally had found anchor. But, the historians now note that Kennedy had before all that drama already approved a nuclear development program at the grand monetary magnitude of 17 billion dollars and announced that the United States would train the new kind of force which would defeat guerrilla warfare. Ho Chi Minh had, after all, humiliated the French in Vietnam with it. The world's largest pool of human bodies, China, had been re-captured by Mao's communists using that same combat technology. The United States would overcome it all with the Green Berets. And, if the Russians had scared Americans (including their leaders) by sending Sputnik (the space satellite), and then Yuri Gagarin (the first Russian (and man) to be sent into space exploration), Kennedy would do the more spectacular landing of man on the moon; and of course, threaten to bomb the Russian

Communists from there if they did not stop frightening the capitalist world. The more Kennedy went into political space flights, the further away he went from the poverty, brutality, and permanent social warfare with which white America had been hounding the lives of their Black countrymen for centuries past.

President-elect Bill Clinton (as of this writing) may be already well onto this policy trail. The signals are familiar. Capitalism's recent flash victory in Eastern Europe and the Soviet Union is in serious trouble. Already, in Lithuania, the Communists have been voted back after the brutal faces of mass poverty were seen looming towards the populace of that little country. The West German strategy of shutting down factories (especially the most viable and competitive ones) in former East Germany, has created mass unemployment whose horrors have been redirected by Helmut Kohl into that old and terrible tide of racism and anti-Semitism. The Yeltsin team in Russia is under threat, and America has become a hated country among ordinary Russians. The Americans may have hoped to conquer the whole of Russia with Coca Cola and hamburgers where German tanks failed to capture Leningrad. If they fail, will they invade and occupy Russia under the name of defending "democratic Yeltsin?" That is one of the big questions flashing across the screens of our tomorrows for Bill Clinton.

Then, there are the Iranians. While Iraq was being bombed with the help of Egypt, Saudi Arabia, and an unprotesting Algeria, the Ayatollahs were rebuilding their religious, economic, and military factories to combat-readiness. Ironically, the IMF and the World Bank were on Iran's side as they battered the economies of Egypt and Algeria with the artillery of structural adjustment. The social welfare policies, which underpinned the popularity of Nasser in Egypt and Boummediene in Algeria, were torpedoed and demolished by the IMF-World Bank brigades. The resultant poverty has now revealed the new governments as enemies of the people. For Egyptians, it has brought back memories of the Ottoman Turks. Nasser had overthrown the Ottoman Turks because they were seen as slavish agents and servants of the British against the interests of Egypt and her people. Tragic how History never seems to learn from History.

The Iranians waited in the shadows and, after Operation Desert Storm (to the Iraqis, Operation Blood Storm) had spent its fury, the Iranians seem to have ignited an Operation Return to Moslem Fundamentals. They have been wrecking politics-as-usual in

Algeria. They have been in Egypt for some time now. The kill-ings of Christian Coptic Egyptians and foreign tourists evoke im-ages of Boutrous Boutrous Ghali (an Egyptian Copt) at the United Nations and of what is seen as American/European re-coloniza-tion of the Middle East. The proposed landing of thirty thousand American troops in Somalia alone may be a Bush-Clinton re-sponse to this scenario. Somalia may prove a terrible graveyard for her tortured citizens, but no matter—it has one vital natural resource which the Americans need: its geographical location. Its northern border overlooks the entry to the Suez Canal, the lifeblood of Egypt, Israel, and Saudi Arabia. Its eastern shores open directly into the international waters of the Indian Ocean—the route to Iran. American bombers from airfields in Somalia and from floating airfields on tops of warships, can hit Iran di-rectly and from short distances as well as shield U.S. allies in the region.

With the coming to power of Al Bashir in Sudan, the Iranians now have a friend on African soil. If they were engineers of the coup that put Al Bashir in power, then their agenda is at an ad-vanced state. This is most awkward for Egypt whose Nile wa-ters pass through the whole length of that vast Sudan (from the Ugandan and Ethiopian borders in the south to the Egyptian bor-der in the north)—a desperate situation of vulnerability for Egypt. What is more irritating for Egyptian leaders is not only that they once shared rulership of Sudan with Britain, but each had its own set of operatives in the politics of the Sudan. Somebody in Cairo went to sleep, and the Ayatollahs crept in unseen, or perhaps scoffed at.[1]

There are also rumblings of the politicization of Islam further south in Kenya, Uganda, and Tanzania. Libya has long been urging Zanzibaris to break off from Tanzania. The Iranians, if views in *African Events* (a magazine financed by Iran) are any indicator, have joined the Libyans in this quest. Again, this is a development which would threaten loyal allies of the West, par-ticularly Kenya and Museveni's Uganda.

The instability in Algeria and Egypt is a blow to Africa's quest for a decade of recovery. These countries have made enormous material and diplomatic contributions to anti-colonial and anti-apartheid struggles for the well-being of Africa. With progress towards the material death of apartheid in sight, their contribu-tion towards the new combat against the International Economic

Apartheid which the West is seeking to consolidate, is urgent and essential. It was Ahmed Ben Bella of Algeria, a Moslem, who urged that all peoples of Africa must die a little so that colonialism and apartheid can finally be defeated. Ben Bella and Nasser never saw Islam as a new weapon for continental instability, bloodshed, and endless destruction of civil society. Their legacies deserve better tribute from African people everywhere.

This will be the consequence if a bitter paradox is enacted by which the negative politicization of Islam across Africa becomes the red carpet on which the Bush-Clinton United States governments will march forth and land in a cruel drama of Pax Americana recolonization of Africa. The Somalis have already paved the way for it in a macabre ritual of clan genocide, which was either unplanned in its origin or is after all a Frankensteinian vision of somebody somwhere in or outside the Middle East.

The challenge for Africa in these circumstances is considerable and multi-dimensional. On the one hand, her new African Diaspora policy of seeking reparations must also put emphasis on the positive realizations of economic, social and political reconstruction of the lives of African-Americans, African-Brazilians, African-Peruvians, African-Caribbeans, etc. For this strategy to work, *Bill* Clinton must be stopped from becoming *Bush* Clinton. Those Americans who earn their daily bread from shares in military-based industries must be stopped from transforming Bill Clinton into Bush-Clinton-Kennedy. Their success in capturing Clinton's hands, if not his imagination, will negate his promise of a new and better home for *all* Americans.

And yet, an answer must be found to the bloody politicization of Islam on the continent as a weapon of diplomatic leadership by extra-African regions and countries. The answer to this problem obviously cannot be new and more American military occupation of Africa. It must be anchored in African occupation of the leadership position in Islam. The largest amount of Moslem space in the world is in Africa: Black and Arab.

It is about time for the historic significance of this fact to be seized by Africans—leaders and non-leaders alike. It is the vast numbers of Moslems in Africa who must assume their historic responsibility of locating Islam within world politics in the coming centuries. Only in this way can we assume Africa's rightful size in our relationship with agents of the looming shadows of the Yankee Eagle and the "Western Asian" Ayottolahs.[2]

Notes

1. In a British Broadcasting Corporation (BBC) interview on April 1, 1993, President Hosni Mubarak of Egypt said "Iran through Sudan, they want to destabilize Egypt so that Iran can gain full control on the Gulf countries....The only obstacle for Iran (they have said) is Egypt and Hosni Mubarak."

2. Mohammed Heikal, *Secret Channels: The Inside Story of Arab-Israeli Peace Negotiations* (London: Harper Collins, 1996) completely ignores the role of Black Africa.

20

ON JESUS' BEING AFRO-JEWISH

Was Jesus of Nazareth an Afro-Jew? The question at once touches on the anthropology of religious ideas and on the history of the Middle East during the over three thousand centuries of Egyptian imperial supremacy and exploitation in that region. Jesus is "African" in his roots in several ways. At a *personal* political level, he had (in his infancy, at least) served a period of political asylum in Egypt in order to escape from Roman colonial plans to slaughter all babies born in his age-grade. As an adult nationalist leader, his challenge of Roman colonial rule over Jews could trace its roots back to Moses' (the son of a Pharaoh and a Jewish mother) rejection of his own paternal roots and assumption of leadership of the Jewish Exodus. To achieve freedom for his people, he ran away from politics, to achieve a Jewish nation-state, he rejected Egyptian citizenship. Jesus sought a return to the nationalism of this Exodus without running away from Israel.[1]

That was Jesus the anti-colonial politician. Having grown up in Egypt, he obviously imbibed her political ideas. Having come from a people who for centuries had lived in Egypt as slaves, he also imbibed those political ideas which were now in their collective memory. And, in particular (so argues the French scholar and Egyptologist, Alexander Moret), they and Jesus had imbibed the notion of the ruler as both God and the Son of God. Divinity was both *profane* in the physical immediacy and tactility of a Pharaoh, and *ultimate* as the celestial father of the Pharaoh sitting in heavenly paradise. To the Egyptians, the awesome arrogance of power was both immediate in its human form and remote in its heavenly location. In asserting that he was the Son of God, Jesus of Nazareth was appropriating for an Israeli nation the same legitimizing principle, which had reigned supreme in Egypt for several millenia. In this sense, he was *Africanizing* both the politics of Israel, and (without knowing it) the central doctrine of Christianity, the movement later built around his person.

But might Jesus also have been *biologically* African too? Slavery, as a social tool, has often that paradoxical achievement of commonalizing both the master male and (more secretly, the master female too) with the slave female and male in the movement of sexual intercourse, and, more importantly, in the subsequent biological contribution of human genes to the children born of these social technologies. If Moses had a pharaoh—a Black man—for a father, Jesus of Nazareth too may have had a Pharaoh Black man as his grandfather or great-great grandfather. If so, then as a Pharaoh he was both a Prince and God. Perhaps, history has often assigned to Afro-Jewish blood the rare responsibilities of producing the political saviors of the Jewish nation-state and of anchoring Christianity.

Up to 1948, a peculiar mixing of the legacies of the Exodus of Moses and the personal exoduses of Jesus of Nazareth (out of Egypt and into death) had resulted in a number of prolonged and terrible persecutions of the Jews by various European peoples amongst whom they found themselves. The most horrendous one was the extermination of six million Jews by Germans, Poles, and others during Hitler's rule. Their persecutors had often justified their beastialities on the claim of punishing the Jews for the historic crime of killing Jesus of Nazareth. In 1948, the "second Jewish Exodus"—out of Europe—led to the creation of the state of Israel. That Exodus has since developed not only a home but a rare, rugged arsenal of power and force in a combative ecology.

The themes of Moses with his Exodus, and Jesus with his Redemption, have assumed rare political analogy among African peoples, particularly those in the Diaspora. The most visible ones have been that of Emperor Haile Selassie of Ethiopia and Marcus Garvey of Jamaica. The Italian invasion of Ethiopia and Haile Selassie's flight to safety in London, promptly turned him in to Jah Rastafarai, the African God and "Jesus" to the Rastas of Jamaica. Marcus Garvey mobilized the Black folks in the United States for a redemption from servitude through an exodus back to Africa. As things later turned out, if Garvey's followers did not succeed in driving European colonialism out of Africa with the black arithmetic of an Exodus, they did obtain a base called Liberia (the land of liberty at the end of the exodus sea journey). Both Haile Selassie's personal flight into political asylum (like Jesus' during his infancy) and Marcus Garvey's redemption of Black Americans out of the fire of slavery into Liberia, were flights in the service of national freedom and independence. Liberia was Africa's Israel for African people in the Americas. Liberia and Israel both received the official endorsement of the political might of the United States, the new superpower.

Yet somehow, Liberia to date has never gotten from successive governments of the United States, the same quality and quantity of material support as Israel has received to date. What Liberia did get was more exploitation—of her rubber, iron ore, and labor. Moreover, when "socialist" agitators under MOJA (Movement for Justice in Africa) got very close to winning power from president Tolbert, United States' officials rushed Samuel Doe into a military coup, and from then on Liberia went into the coma of the decay and collapse of the nation-state. An African exodus had crashed against the indifferent boulders of time and change.

The tribulations of Israel (war in 1948, war in 1967, war in 1973, Desert Storm in 1990/1991, the Intifada struggle of the Palestinians) have received consistently resolute United States support as well as more intensive presence economically and militarily in the Middle East. Israel, herself, has matured beyond the siege mentality of the first three decades after 1948, and is currently negotiating with the Arabs from a position of power and national self-confidence.

The year 1992 was one of mayhem in Liberia. Somebody has poured a lot of fuel into Charles Taylor's ambitions for military seizure of power. The inferno has been very successful in diverting Nigeria's military resources into Liberia. Or rather, *away from* Somalia and Angola. Somehow, while Liberia failed to attract open United States military resources, Somalia has done so as of the first week of December 1992. Was this the indifferent hand of time and change again at work, or of a willful computer program? Did Africa's intervention into the legacy of exodus out of America trap Africa into a pre-planned quagmire so that the United States would be free to organize a military *inxodus* into Somalia? Was the American *inxodus* yet again another detail in her protection of the legacy of Moses' Exodus?

The Italian invasion of Ethiopia turned Haile Selassie into an African Jesus for oppressed peoples of African descent in the Americas. Freedom from internal colonialism as well as general European colonial domination of Africans everywhere became their new war songs. Will the American *inxodus* in the service of "Restoring Hope" to starving and lawless Somalia also arouse new demands for freedom from centuries of starvation and indignities endured by African and indigenous Red Indian peoples in Brazil, Colombia, Ecuador, Peru, etc.? If it does and the United States responds as she has done in Israel, then the question about Jesus being Afro-Jewish will have new and significant echoes in the Americas of the 21st Century.

Notes

1.   Cheik Anta Diop, in UNESCO, *The Peopling of Ancient Egypt and the Deciphering of Meoroitic Script* (Paris, 1978).

21

WOODROW WILSON, NATIONALISMS, AND JONAS SAVIMBI

Woodrow Wilson, President of the United States of America in 1917, made the following euphoric statement to the American Congress in that year:

> Does not every American feel that assurance has been added to our hope for the future peace of the world by the wonderful and heartening things that have been happening within the last few weeks in Russia? Russia was known by those who knew her best to have been always in fact democratic at heart, in the vital habits of her thought, in all the intimate relationships of her people that spoke their natural instinct, their habitual attitude towards life. The autocracy that crowned the summit of her political structure, long as it has stood and terrible as was the reality of its power, was not in fact Russian in origin, character or purpose; and now it has been shaken off, and the great,

generous Russian people have been added in all their naive majesty and might to the forces that are fighting for
freedom in the world, for justice and for peace.[1]

The enemy of freedom between 1914 and 1917 was German
nationalism. Soon after the defeat of the Germans, the new Russian friends of Wilson's "Justice and....peace" in the world, the
communist Bolsheviks, were to become America's mortal enemies until the period 1939 to 1945 when German "National
Socialism" (Nazism) under Adolf Hitler came back to reclaim its
rightful place in world history as America's enemy of "freedom
in the world." If Hitler had not been stupid enough to want to
conquer for himself that vast land of Russia as the biggest single
and united colony in world history, the colonies he had already
conquered in Europe might have been Germany's for some decades after 1945. Nor would the Russian Communists have re-
gained their notorious title in the eyes of America and her NATO
allies as the enemies of "justice" in the world, nor have retained it
from 1945 to 1991.

German nationalism had grown out of severe inferiority complexes, bred by comparison with the French, the British, and the
Southern European races who claimed the learning and civiliza-
tions of Ancient Greece and Rome as their ancestry. The Germanic races were the barbarians. German thinkers like Goethe
knew that Greece and Rome had in fact learned all their mathematics, architecture, medicine, and literature from the Ancient
Egyptians; they therefore sought to claim that the Ancient Egyptians were a Germanic people, but when the evidence that the
Ancient Egyptians had been Black Africans could not be denied,
they gave up and ran to India. If only they could claim plausibly
that the Aryan races who created the Sanskrit civilization in India
were their true ancestors, then German pride, patriotism, and nationalism would have a source different and "superior" to the
legacies of Greece and Rome. Between 1939 and 1945, German
tanks and bombers blasted this message savagely across Europe.
Since 1992, it has been the German national currency and industrial economic might doing the blasting. As to whether the Russian Communists under Gorbachev saw this coming, and chose
to become America's friends of "freedom in the world" (this time
without losing two hundred million people to a new barbarism of
German nationalism), we can only speculate.

Similar inferiority complexes, which also stirred up German nationalism under another climate, formed the bedrock of Boer nationalism in South Africa from 1652 to at least 1961 (when Prime Minister Verwoerd was forced to carry South Africa out of the British Commonwealth). From being the wretched lot of sailors from Holland (and in later years also from France and Germany), the Boer small farmers held on to their dream of the promised land proclaimed for them in the Bible as the "land of milk and honey at the source of River Nile." When some of them finally saw a river in today's Transvaal, they thanked the Lord. Their dream was, however, constantly overshadowed by the military power of the Zulu, Soto, and other African Empires they met.[2] Later, aristocrats from Britain (who financed the hunt for colonial supervision over gold and diamonds found under these lands) soon caught up with them. No matter how far into the vast lands (beyond the Cape of Good Hope) the Boers ran, the British industrialists, bankers, and traders—gobblers of empires—caught up with them and imposed colonial rule over them. In comparison to the British, the Boers were a wild, illiterate, backward lot. Inferiority complexes and resentments deepened and fueled a profound Boer nationalism of tribal resentment and self-contempt. The only concession the British made to the Boer was to team up with him militarily and politically against the African peoples of South Africa. That collusion ensured a vast slave labor force for both the British industrialist and the Boer.

The Boer also had the defeated Africans to despise by way of compensation. The primitiveness, which underlies a nationalism born of inferiority complexes, is often virulent. It made Germans turn six million Jews into human waste and experimental data. Previously, before being defeated in 1917, Germans had slaughtered over four million Africans in Namibia. The Boer's record in South Africa achieved levels of racist stupidity such as the Pretoria government (even at the height of its diplomatic "offensive" aimed at making friends in Africa), accepting only a white British businessman as Malawi's first ambassador to South Africa.

Jonas Savimbi's ethnic nationalism is born of severe inferiority complexes in a "bush people" towards the "civilized evoluées" of Luanda comprising the first African ethnic groups to enjoy what little Portuguese education there was under five hundred years of domination. It appeared that some Africans actually only enjoyed the status of partakers of slum-dweller civilization in Luanda, Benguela, and Lobito. Whether Augustinho Neto set up his medical clinic in the slum area of Luanda and from that socio-geographical point realized that only an anti-colonial struggle based on mobilizing the angers and hungers of those slum masses across all ethnic lines could succeed, and did in fact build MPLA on that basis, is of no material value in countering ethnic impulses rooted in inferiority complexes. To Savimbi, the MPLA (especially the intellectuals and their mass following on the Atlantic coast) represents a historical attitude, an existential space and reflex towards his peoples of the hinterland. To cooperate with them, to accept a political reality of popular acceptance, which they have created and which justifies their assumption of power, is for Savimbi to experience a psychic death, a personality suicide. This is a spatial irrationality in the mind, which precludes politics and statesmanship. It is a condition of total psychological violence towards the "other." It is here that Savimbi and the Boer leaders (from Malan in 1948 to Botha in 1990) meet in a moment of similarity. It is here that Savimbi and Helmut Kohl of West Germany meet when Kohl decided to offer East Germans other racial groups (i.e, those from Angola, Mozambique and Vietnam who had originally come to East Germany as communist ideological friends) as emotional targets for violence and hate in order to escape from the ancient German nationalism.

Where does all this leave President Woodrow Wilson and his Russian friends of "freedom in the world?" The Bolsheviks had also been spurred on by deep inferiority complexes towards the Western Europeans. The industrial revolution, first of Britain, then France, and then Germany, had left czarist Russia behind as a backward rural empire. The attitudes of superiority, which accompanied this economic advancement in Western Europe, even infected Karl Marx and his thesis that socialism and freedom from human want would explode with blood out of the pregnant womb of developed capitalism (that is to say, from the genius of the Western European). When Lenin and the Bolsheviks struck in 1917 and set out to build socialism from the backwaters of civilization, a crucial part of their reflex was their resentment of the contempt with which Western European marxists treated Russia despite her vast size. Was it this nationalism of anti-Europeanism, this Russian rejection of Europe's claim to being the superior primary herdsman of History and Human Destiny, which Woodrow Wilson hailed in 1917? If that is so, then America's "friend of freedom" was a nationalism born of inferiority complexes. Is that perhaps what the later American presidents after Woodrow Wilson—particularly those from J.F. Kennedy to George Bush—also came to value in apartheid as political expression of Boer nationalism at its most barbaric and industrially advanced stage from 1960 to 1990 and later in Jonas Savimbi's UNITA? Yet, in both cases, they were supported as part of America's strategy of opposition to Soviet imperialism in Africa. With Russian nationalism in the 1990s resting on a super-industrial base, and with Boer nationalism also now on its own relatively developed ethnic industrial base, does Savimbi's ethnic nationalism (with a dependent military arsenal but without a developed industrial base) now suddenly find itself without American courters precisely because America's idea of "freedom in the world" has never embraced nationalisms based only on inferiority complexes, without a significant economic market and impulse?

Yet, being without Boer or Yankee devoted lovers will not make Savimbi's complexes go away. It may simply make them more desperate and available to political pimps like the Italian Mafia, who will still want to sell guns and bombs so long as Savimbi can lay his hands on diamonds in Zaire (now Congo) and Northern Angola. The Mafia have no visible embassies and no visible seats at the United Nations. They have no visible nationalism to promote. It is for this scenario of bestial degeneration outside of the realm of politics that African diplomacy must urgently face Savimbi's illness and turn to the medicines of traditional African statecraft for the task of exercising that evil spirit out of UNITA. These same medicines will also be vitally needed for handling the least educated and economically less well-off Boers in today's South Africa. Likewise for today's Bantustan officials. They too have, for decades, had only inferiority complexes to live on. Woodrow Wilson's legacy offers little help or hope.

Yet, the United States has her own record of a democracy with severe internal oppression of her Black citizens with population sizes larger than many nations with seats at the United Nations. It has also supported the most brutal, corrupt, and dictatorial regimes in South America, Zaire, and Idi Amin's Uganda.

Memories, especially those of governments and nations, do not go away. Boris Yeltsin must be cursing the West for delaying his impulse to hang Gorbachev. Jonas Savimbi's cancer in Angola must not be allowed more time to metastasize. And African political diplomacy (based on the combination of Mugabe-Nkomo and Diof-Wade, neodiarchy at the top) as well as the demand for payment of war-reparations from South Africa and the United States (for reconstruction of the Angola they openly helped UNITA to destroy) must be put on track. The impression that African blood can be shed and African economies ruined with impunity must be eradicated. If Savimbi hoodwinks the electorate into voting him in, or rather into not turning out to vote in MPLA's Dos Santos, Africa will witness perhaps the most murderous dictatorship yet.

Mr. Savimbi is demanding veto power over the elections and policies in Angola not for the benefit of the people of that country, but for that of former president De Klerk and the whites of South Africa. De Klerk must show the white electorate that this is Savimbi's way of paying them back for the blood of all those thousands of white South African soldiers who died fighting for UNITA against Cuban and MPLA soldiers. De Klerk can then turn to Mandela and argue that if the ANC does not abandon policies aimed at satisfying the exploding economic expectations of the Black majority, the South Africa armed forces and the Afrikaaner right wing will not accept future "free and fair election" testified to by international witnesses if ANC wins, with its commitment to taking back the 87% of the land and 100% of industry and the national bureaucracy, etc. now held by the whites before 1994.[3]

Notes

1. Alexander Steward, *The World, the West and Pretoria* (New York: David Mckay co., 1977) discusses Wilsonian ideas of self-determination with considerable resentment insofar as it incited African nationalism in his own country towards South Africa.

2. T. Dunbar Moodie, *The Rise of Afrikanerdom: Power, Apartheid, and the Afrikaaner Civil Religion* (University of California

Press, Berkeley,1975) quotes Malan as saying, "It is through the will of God that the Afrikaaner people exists at all ....God willed that the Afrikaaner People should be continually threatened by other peoples. There was the ferocious barbarian who resisted the intruding Christian civilization and caused the Afrikaaner's blood to flow in streams. There were times when as a result of this, the Afrikaner was deeply despairing, but God at the same time prevented the swamping of the young Afrikaner people in the sea of barbarism" (p. 248).

3. Sam C. Nolutshungu, *South Africa in Africa : A Study of Ideology and Foreign Policy*; (Manchester University, 1975), documents South Africa's economic, political, and espionage activities across Southern Africa. He quoted president Kenneth Kaunda's speech to the United Nations General Assembly thus: "*Apartheid* is on the offensive...The Boer trek is on and is now instrumental to the wider concept of neo-colonialism" (p.226).

22

AFRICA'S EXPECTATIONS OF BILL CLINTON

"Saddam Hussein voted with his Mother of all Silences and President Bush crashed in the loudest political humiliation in recent American politics. Saddam would not even be provoked into lifting an eyebrow at Turkish troops sent into Iraq last week by a desparate Jim Baker (former Secretary of State turned Bush's campaign manager)."[1] So said a celebrant. He also had a prepared list of spirits of the dead ranged against Bush. There were the angry spirits of Somalis who had died in the late 1970s in a futile Ogaden War as agents of American foreign policy bent on routing out the Soviet-backed Mengistu regime in Ethiopia, and was the beginning of the present tragedy reigning over that poor country. There is the angry ghost of Tito whose country's non-aligned policy had always been celebrated as a brave stand against communist Russia. No sooner had he gone than the West hungrily fanned the fires of tribalism to the present ruin of his dear Yugoslavia. Then, there are the livid spirits of Jewish victims of

the Nazi holocaust who watched President Bush stand by in silence as leaders of reunited Germany systematically rekindled
hatred against Jews and other races. My friend's list of dead
enemies of President Bush's re-election was seemingly endless.
Maybe he had a point but there are other equally impatient anti-
Bush campaigners who deserve our attention.

President Bush is a child of material and psychological privi-
leges who saw the opportunity to rule America and her empire as
his right. He graduated from Yale, a school with a tradition of
providing the leadership of the almost omnipotent Central Intelligence Agency (CIA). Global in reach, the CIA, since the World
War II, developed in the 1960s the attitude of seeing nothing sacred in other people's nationalisms and the visions of their best
leaders, if American national interest said so. From kidnapping
and murdering Patrice Lumumba in 1961, to the invasion of
Panama and the capture and export of its leader, General Manuel
Noriega in 1989, there runs a thread of institutional consistency
of method. From persistent efforts to kill Fidel Castro with poi-
soned cigars, to luring Saddam Hussein into invading Kuwait
only to blast Iraq into chemical mud, an attitude of imperial arrogance and ruthlessness is manifest. This was the attitude that
nurtured George Bush from the directorship of the CIA to the
presidency of the United States. Despite the fact that he had
lately been his country's ambassador to China, it was he who
presided over the "pro-democracy" invasion of that country, pushing China into turning its sickle on its own dear youth. Bush was
the last of the Cold War hammers, which the United States churned
out as its leaders.

During the later part of the campaign, President Bush remarked
that he had not gone to Oxford as Bill Clinton did. He intended
the remark as a sneer but it registered as an exercise in self-pity.
It was an echo of that quality of "excellence" which Bush so
prized but now seemed to miss sorely. It was something that
neither his Yale certificate nor his money as a millionaire, nor
even his power as an incumbent President could ever conjure.
Its elusiveness was its nasty sting, especially since Clinton had
also been at Yale Law School at some point.

But, perhaps there was something else in the circumstances
that took Bill Clinton to Oxford that irked Bush. Clinton went to
Oxford as a Rhodes Scholar, the scholarship program willed by
Cecil Rhodes—the man who dreamed of a British empire which

would run from the Cape of Good Hope to Cairo; the man after whom Rhodesia (now Zimbabwe) was named; the man whose legacy was "the best and the brightest" in each generation of an imperial power studying together and together creating new dreams of new frontiers of human achievements. This tradition of lofty dreams may have been what was missing from George Bush's own upbringing at Yale, with its emphasis on raw and muscular might; of cigarette lighters exploding as bombs over the beards of a Fidel Castro; of tracking down with the help of satellites such visionary men as Che Guevera, reducing them to the common status of a wild rhino or a prowling leopard; of guided missiles exploding inside the nostrils of an Iraqi baby in a Baghdad home. Faced with a Bill Clinton who churned out words of prophecy and visions of a redeemed American people, *here and now*, President Bush perhaps felt the rigidities in his Cold War elbows, unable to respond to Clinton's call for *the human spirit as a new frontier* for the new and moral American to conquer and seize.

The signals were clear but bizarre for George Bush as President. First, a brilliant young woman with a face as calm as a blue sky sits day after day inside American television sets clanging word-swords with a male-dominated panel of congressmen. Her name, Anita Hill. Black and beautiful. Challenging the *moral* (not legal and political) credentials of a *black* (not white) man nominated to the Supreme Court by George Bush. She was more than a pretty face. She was a young professor of law at a leading American university, very blue in the color of her brain she was, and is.

President Bush and his advisers did not realize that Anita Hill had launched a political brushfire that would arouse a profound political indignation and combativeness in American women. "Congress," the women fumed, "is dominated by men who have no understanding of the color of terror, which the American woman lives with from birth to death. This must change. More women must stand for elections to Congress and be voted for. Power understands only power." While this anger was flaming all around him, George Bush was preaching about "family values" accusing Clinton of adultery; getting the State Department to investigate Clinton's mother and posing as an anti-abortionist while showing a rare indifference to AIDS, a great scare to women. The VOA reporters who relayed George Bush's voice acknowledging defeat, followed it up with the news report that the first

African-American woman had been elected to the U.S. Senate from the State of Illinois. Talk about not being familiar with the contours of visions, and Bush displayed it.

Another bizarre event exploded in Los Angeles. Four white policemen beat a Black man, Rodney King (who had committed no grave offense), until he became a cripple. Somebody recorded the event on a video and gave it to a television station. That drama of official racist savagery was beamed across America and the world over and over again. A predominantly middle-class, (i.e, suburban) white jury found the policemen not guilty of any crime. George Bush was silent even though the event came soon after Black American soldiers had just been shown over and over again on television as war heroes in the Gulf War. Anger exploded in the streets. The official figures probably downplayed the numbers of people shot and killed by the police, as well as by angry rioters. European radio stations, probably urged by new fears of American domination of Europe (now that the USSR was no more), reported the tragedy with self-righteous indignation, preaching an inward gaze at Bush. President Bush provided no alternative agenda for a baffled and shamefaced nation caught nude in a ritual dance of blood-letting. The reports of his defeat also carried tidings of more African-Americans and Hispanics elected to the new American Congress.

Finally, the rewards to Americans for the "death of communism" came in an atavistic panorama. Blood from "ethnic cleansing" from former Yugoslavia (once a celebrated ally of the West) had been relentless; the new empire of exported democracy was bringing unending television pictures of officially sponsored slaughters in South Africa; and the reunification of Germany (the ultimate triumph of Western democracy) had turned severely painful for the four million Jews in New York alone as Germans reverted quickly into the old primitive vision of anti-semitism. From Georgia to Uzbekistan, the new democracy had metamorphosed into *bloodocracy* as mayhem now stood between the borders of Russia and her neighbors. It was a cheerless world which urged Americans to ask uneasy questions about the glories of their country's foreign policy. Painful doubts combined with the economic death of the middle-class (which started with Reagan's Presidency) to produce a yearning for a new voice at the top; a new frontier inside the kitchens of middle-class parents. This was a mood, which George Bush, the clandestine imperial gladiator from Yale, the millionaire, could not easily sense, let alone comprehend, with a flexing of the muscles of his heart.

Mwalimu Nyerere once said that the fact that the peasant is poor does not make him a natural socialist. Bill Clinton was mocked by President Bush for coming from the most backward state in the United States. Perhaps, that may have given Clinton a sobering realization that a large section of his countrymen and women live in America's own Third World in the ghettos, the poor rural South, and Midwestern states. That in battering at the wall of apartheid in South Africa, Brazil, Colombia, Guatemala, etc, the United States is also condemning to extinction the *de facto* apartheid, which cuts off West and South Chicago from the white parts of the city and its wealth in the suburbs; battering dreams of its African-American inhabitants with alcoholism, drugs, and self-hate. That the Japanese racists may have a point after all when their leaders have attributed the economic and technological fatigue of the United States to her wastage through racial deprivation of its African-American population. And that wastage has gone on now for over four hundred years.

Perhaps Clinton will easily appreciate the simple economic law that capitalist production requires effective markets and consumers, not only in the recession now gripping Britain, Europe, and the United States, but in Africa too, whose markets are daily being bled by terrible debt repayments. That the IMF's Structural Adjustment Program in Africa cannot be regarded as the equivalent of the terrible human costs exacted from European workers during the industrial revolution. There are no African industries yet, only the shallow footholds of subsidiaries of multinational corporations. The deaths of African children denied access to health care; the blockage of African childen with no schools to attend; the mental and physical distortions of malnourished African children—all these sacrifices are in vain, and not a necessary price for industrial savings and reinvestment. It is a blockage of development.

Perhaps Clinton will learn to accept the fact that the Black man in Cuba has lived a life superior to all his brethren in the rest of the world because of Castro's socialist vision and practices; that the Soviet Union has left behind a legacy of service and uplift for the ordinary citizen and his children (which capitalism has painfully failed to achieve in Western Europe and North America) which should be part of our collective human infrastructures as we move into the twenty-first century. In Africa, the MPLA in Angola, FRELIMO in Mozambique, the PAIGC in Guinea, the ANC in South Africa, FNL in Algeria, SWAPO in Namibia, ZANU PF in Zimbabwe, and TANU in Tanzania, have brought with them legacies of whole peoples being aroused into collective politics calling for profound sacrifices across decades of struggle for the sake of destroying old colonial politics of historic selfishness and despicably cruel inhumanity of man. They have brought forth, out of the muck and grime of centuries of colonial rule, rare men and women (Amilcar Cabral, Samora Machel, Augustinho Neto, Sam Nujoma, Nelson Mandela, Mwalimu Nyerere, Winnie Mandela, Miriam Makeba, etc.) whose qualities of selfless fortitude and total dedication to the advancement of human freedom and dignity have enriched our civilization and humanity's collective pool of daring and achievement. These sterling themes must not be scoffed at, or cynically and vindictively mangled and suffocated by power in the service of profit. They are Africa's contribution to humanity's infrastructures for the twenty-first century. America's commitment to freedom and democracy must accord them dignified recognition and not treat them with contemptuous disregard and brutalizing assault.

Perhaps Clinton's call to Americans to give and not always take, to share and not always gather for oneself, will inform his foreign policy too. We, in Africa, have always been taken from; always had the industrial and technological powers of our minerals, our botanical plants, our cotton, cocoa, and rubber (etc.) *not shared with us*; not recycled into our own economies. We, like the rest of the world, have a right to expect a new humanized vision from President Bill Clinton.

Notes

1.   A. Mammoh, *Citizens*, Volume 4, No.33, p.50.

23

"DO NOT WEEP FOR ME"
—LUMUMBA

A voice has asserted that Zaire killed politics in Africa. She became independent on June 30,1960. Four days later, she experienced a creeping military coup, which evolved from soldiers (in a sponsored plan) erupting in a carnival of riotous and brutal mutiny in Kinshasha; to Kasavubu (the figurehead president of the country) dismissing Lumumba from Prime Ministership; to Lumumba counter-dismissing Kasavubu; to Mobutu's soldiers imprisoning Lumumba in his own house and eventually (on January 17, 1961) having him murdered during a picnic. At that picnic of assassination were Moise Tshombe (who had declared Katanga's secession), Godfrey Munongo (Tshombe's Minister of Internal Affairs), and Belgian military officers. Tshombe apparently kicked and jumped on Lumumba's chest and stomach (breaking his ribs); Munongo stabbed Lumumba whose hands were tied behind his back; and a Belgian officer finally shot Lumumba in the head. A Belgian military officer shot Lumumba in the head at point-blank range—the head which contained that lethal pepper-soup of anti-colonialism and African nationalism, the container of the word, that omnipotent carrier of the world's most successful religious and political doctrines. The Belgian military officer hoped to assassinate The Word and that type of African politician who is the purveyor of African nationalism.

Distinguished scholars of Zairian affairs (including Professor Crawford Young) are rather cheeky in singing that politicians killed politics in Zaire (from independence in 1960 to Mobutu's final coming in 1965). They chant that Kasavubu unconstitutionally dismissed Lumumba (thus disgracing both the offices of president and prime minister); that Tshombe fell for the cynical pamperings of racist and imperialist Belgians, South African whites, Britons, and Americans, and declared himself a puppet president of an independent Katanga (thus beginning a balkanization, which was quickly followed by a Baluba State in Kasai, etc.). They beat drums about politicians selling shifting coalition votes for fast monies (thus desecrating the sacred bond of representation of the will of the mass voting public). It all sounds so despicable: the childish Africans at their best. But, well hidden from view are the *invisible hands* of ruthless global power actors.

Lumumba committed the fatal blunder of believing that the United Nations was a body of nations in a global union of consciences, which would condemn and expel Belgian brigandry, piracy, and wanton invasion of his four-day-old independent country. He was naive enough to believe that troops from Ghana serving under the United Nations were Ghanaian African patriots commanded by the powerful Osagyefo, Kwame Nkrumah. As it turned out, they were commanded by General Alexander, a Briton appointed by Nkrumah but who took his orders from the British Ambassador in Leopoldville (Kinshasha). It was these Ghanaian troops which were used by "The Invisible Hands" to prevent Lumumba from using his national radio to broadcast to his people, tell them his version of political truths and mobilize them against the foreign invaders behind Kasavubu and Mobutu. The saddest part of this comedy was that on August 8, 1960, Nkrumah and Lumumba had signed a "secret agreement" in Accra in which they "decided to establish a Union of African States," consisting of their own two countries.[1]

"The Invisible Hands" physically attacked members of parliament. The majority (who supported Lumumba) were prevented from travelling out of Kinshasha to their constituencies and their allowances were stopped (to force them into becoming available for American dollars). On December 1, 1960, Lumumba was arrested. According to the Moroccan Ambassador, "the next morning, a hundred soldiers with helmets and submachine guns at the ready and an old tank with a rusty gun were stationed in front of the Parliament building. The elected representatives of the people were not allowed to enter and continue their deliberations and carry out their tasks." Fifteen provincial parliamentarians, who were supporters of Lumumba, were murdered in Kasai. It sounds familiar today. Mobutu has a longer memory than pro-democracy backers of his current opponents. In short, it was not the politicians in parliament and provincial assemblies who killed politics. Rather, that honor falls to the Belgians, the Americans, the Britons, and the French.

The politician in Africa has generally had bad press. Take the best of them. Samora Machel, Augustinho Neto, Amilcar Cabral, Robert Mugabe, Ahmed Ben Bella, and Sam Nujoma led the most horrendous and daunting national liberation wars in the longest and worst exploited and often least developed colonies in the world. And they did not give up. But there is silence about them now. Kenneth Kaunda and Mwalimu Nyerere often initiated and supported liberation struggles in Mozambique, Zimbabwe, Angola, Namibia, and South Africa. Their reward became the constant propagandistic celebration of their countries (by the Western press) as "among the world's poorest nations." Their tragic trading of relatively toothless (even if politically and militarily very damaging) support for Biafra in return for Euro-American restraint of Portugal and South Africa from full-scale invasions of their very weak countries has, to many, overshadowed their other achievements. The Euro-Americans were, in the end, to encourage South Africa's financing of Kaunda's political electoral defeat, humiliation, and exit; while using in their television newsreels only camera shots, which played down the collective weeping of a spontaneous mass public who lined routes for miles to wave farewell to a voluntarily departing Nyerere. His rare skill in grooming a whole generation of his successors, as well as defeat of tribalism and religious bigotry, continue to receive little attention.

In far away Senegal and Guinea, the two veteran political theorists, Leopold Sedar Senghor and Ahmed Sekou Toure, had even poorer exits. Senghor was disgraced by the French Government getting the Paris-based *Le Monde* newspaper to be the first to carry the announcement of his exit as the way of informing his own subjects in Senegal. The irritated and insulted Senegalese elite responded with the official *Le Soleil* using a farewell picture of Senghor looking away towards his real home in France. His political achievements as a Christian politician ruling a people for twenty five years who are ninety percent Moslem, even if at the expense of repressing their Wolof identity and cultural expression, were played down. Sekou Toure, the socialist, had to die in capitalist America, in a seeming final and opportunistic bow to the superiority of capitalist technology in medical care (even though he was already unconscious when the decision to fly him to the United States was taken). His murder of Diallo Telli (the first Secretary General of the OAU) and hundreds of Guinea's intellectuals and technocrats overshadowed a novel attempt to create a nation with a dignified people (from under decades of French racist contempt) as well as marry socialist principles with the ancient community solidarity of non-feudal peoples of Guinea.

Balewa, Nkrumah, and Obote are presented more as politicians who ignored the gun to their peril. Not as rare men from minority tribes (located in the educationally and economically least developed zones of their respective countries) who had turned these liabilities into assets for the deconstruction of colonially structured inequalities (and hostilities) and selfless construction of nationhood. Balewa and Nkrumah are blamed for not properly reading the meaning (for their own troops serving in Zaire) of Euro-American secret services' use of Mobutu to overthrow and brutally murder Lumumba—a popularly elected politician. The list continues. Both the purveyor and the word in Africa are currencies which have been constantly devalued by Euro-American power markets. The celebration of nationalist heroes and African ideologies is apparently over and gone. Even "democracy" is not new to the continent. The new import is "pro-democracy," which is supposedly superior to old "African elders talking and talking until reaching their agreed consensus."

Physically too, the Nationalist anti-colonial politician is a vanishing breed. Presidents Banda in Malawi and Houphuet Boigny in Cote d'Ivoire were recent species, historic carriers of an ancient mission. Nyerere, Kaunda, Senghor, Obote, Nelson Mandela, and Nnamdi Azikiwe are still around in varying degrees of political animation. But the successor African politicians (steeped in the silence of military rule) have probably committed the terrible error of losing their heroes under dark covers of decades-long political nights. They have written no biographies of African nationalist politicians, villains and master crafts-men alike. They have sponsored no media interviews or scholarly studies of those now departed to the ethereal zone of the ancestors, nor even of those still alive (whether out of or still in power). It is as if the "old" and "new breed" politicians will come as maggots out of the historical dungheap of military romance with Euro-American invisible hands, rather than as seedlings sprouting out of old dried seed made wet by downpours of civilian and military statecraft, tribulations and sometimes rare imagination. If this be so, then the "pro-democracy" Euro-American sponsored politicians in Africa will be today's civilian versions of yesterday's Mobutu; yet more killers of The Word (as a being on its own trajectory across Africa), and of its historic medium, orator, and actor. Such a situation is clearly unsatisfactory. Among other things, it cripples the pursuit of the "Sankofa" imperative to return to that past halo, flare, and dignity of nationalist politics as a vocation in selfless search for the humanity and collective betterment of a people ill-served by recent world history.

The case can be presented without polemics. Today's African public requires positive emotions and images from memories of the nationalist politicians. Today's politicians need chlorinated noise pools for washing off three decades of militarization encrusted on the mass public. The stormy impact of Spike Lee's film about the combative nationalist politics of the African-American firebrand Malcolm X on the Black youth in the Americas and Britain, suggests that films titled Kwame, Amilcar, Samora, Malam, Mwalimu, and Ziki may bring back some life-force to the African politician mummy.

Notes

1. Kwame Nkrumah, *Challenge of the Congo* (London: Panaf Books, 1974).With growing exasperation and helplessness Nkrumah ends up characterizing Lumumba as "impulsive."

24

BEYOND BOUTROUS BOUTROUS GHALI'S EYEBROWS

"The fact that no woman has hitherto been a candidate for the (United Nations) Secretary Generalship is grotesque, especially for an organization whose Charter commits it to the equality of men and women."[1]

So say the authors of a 1990 study jointly sponsored by the Dag Hammarskjold Foundation and the Ford Foundation. Before the assumption of that post by Boutrous Boutrous Ghali from the African continent, that "grotesque" bias would have rung political bells across the continent. The other candidates with complaints against this 47-year-old bias are China, the former USSR, the USA, Britain, France, and the former West Germany. The occupation of the post by Uthant of Burma after the death of Hammarskjold in 1961 in a plane crash in Southern Africa, gave the Asian region (which includes Japan) their chance in the post. Communist China had been denied membership of the United

Nations from 1949 (when Mao's Communist Red Army took power there) to 1972, when with the support of Africa and the Non-Aligned Movement, the Country was given membership. President Nixon will always remember television pictures of Salim Salim, the current OAU Secretary General (at the time Tanzania's Ambassador to the United Nations) dancing in the aisles of the General Assembly after the scoreboard showed that a majority of countries had voted for China's admission against the objections of the United States Government. But, it was also the same President Nixon who was to become the first American President to visit China and shake hands with the awesome and venerable Chairman Mao. Pakistan had been secretly linking Henry Kissinger, Nixon's National Security Advisor, with Chinese officials long before the vote at the United Nations.

The other countries, notably the USA, Britain, France, and the Soviet Union (now reduced to only Russia), have not occupied this post or presented candidates because of an informal agreement that the Secretary General would "not be a national of one of the five permanent Members of the Security Council." Moreover, although the Secretary General is appointed by the UN General Assembly, he has to be presented to the General Assembly by the permanent members of the Security Council.

A candidate who is vetoed by a Permanent Member of the Security Council cannot make it beyond that diplomatic cooking pot. It is so nice a way to own a Secretary General without him being one of your citizens. Boutrous Ghali came from Africa, but he listened more intently to cataracts in the voices of BBC, VOA, Radio France, Radio Moscow and Radio Beijing broadcasters than to those of African radio broadcasters.

The right to exercise the veto power over the choice of a UN Secretary General was proposed by the Soviet Union and accepted by the others. The death of the Soviet Union now allows for the opportunity for members of the General Assembly (especially the tiny countries, Gamba, Kuwait, Rwanda, Panama, Bhutan, Nepal, Luxembourg, Fiji, etc.) to demand the abandonment of this negative power. Africa's Salim Salim was vetoed by the United States, while his opponent was vetoed by China (on behalf of Africa). The power of numbers by small and weak African countries was no match for the vast economic and continental size of the veto-wielding United States.

It was at the first UN General Assembly session (which the British hosted in London in 1946) that the law of the politics of the appointment of the Secretary General was taken. It said, "the first Secretary General be appointed for a term of five years," with the appointment "being open at the end of that period for a further five-year term." This was the second silent power of the veto holders. They elect the man, then excite and animate the wheels of ambition inside his ego and soul for re-election. "He that eats alone, finds no one to bury him when he dies," says an African proverb. The Secretary General builds his infrastructure of assistants. They too begin to see their ambitions dancing on the lake inside his eyes and begin sharpening their personal and collective wits for their man's re-election, or rather, the re-election of their bureaucratic tribe.

In so doing, the walls thicken of the political prison of working "in the knowledge that the Secretary General's chances of re-election would be small if he were to incur the displeasure of one of the permanent members."

Boutrous Boutrous Ghali (and the Africa that sponsored him) was historic in getting elected, as well as in the timing of his entry at the moment of the death of the Cold War. Then there was the birth of three new wars; the Pro-Democracy War which killed the Soviet Union, the Economic War between the United States against Germany and Japan, and the Debt War a.k.a. Dis-development War by the West against Africa. A BBC news broadcast on April 12, 1993, talked of a new report by the African Development Bank which stated that Africa did not experience economic growth, but underwent dis-development. The debt burden and the very low world prices for Africa's agricultural and mineral exports (particularly oil and copper) were blamed. Also blamed was Africa's indulgence in sex and popping out babies who still ate food. The effects of the Debt and Pro-Democracy Wars have saturated global communication. Television pictures of European savagery in the Balkans and parts of the former Soviet Union have competed with African butchery in Liberia, Rwanda, Angola, Mozambique, and Somalia. The return of raw hatreds of other races and peoples have come out of Germany, France, Italy, and Spain in reactions against a phenomenon of vast population movements from Eastern Europe into paradises in the capitalist West long promised by Radio Free Europe and other tools of anti-Communist propaganda over the last forty years.

The chilling cruelties by Croats, Bosnian Moslems, and Bosnian Serbs, have competed across posh living rooms in Tokyo, Sao Paulo, Ottawa, and Paris with those in the streets and slums of South Africa. Somalia, Southern Sudan, Liberia, and Rwanda have exported horrors of human wastage and degradation as consequences of African political failure in the craft of governance.

Boutrous Ghali inherited several global problems. Several of them are truly "phenomena that transcend national boundaries." Technology in "miracle economies" of South Korea, Singapore, Taiwan, and Japan in Asia; the United States, Canada, and Brazil in the Americas; and Germany, France, and Britain in Western Europe, have created new dangers and benefits. Television pictures can now show doctors the working of organs inside their patients—the rich ones, that is, who can pay for such services. Global satellites tell of mineral deposits under the earth in any country in the world, and under the oceans too. Computers in conference with other computers are now discussing problems far too complex for the human brain to cut through. On the negative list is the tyranny of nuclear waste which refuse to have their terrible powers silenced by those who released them for (among other things) killing other human beings. The common heritages of mankind (like the ocean floors and the skies) have become new granaries for chemical toxins no longer wanted by factories, and poisoning seafood eaten by man. British intelligence officers can now record the intimate family chats of their own royalty and leak the information out to newspapers, thus telling other governments that the privacy of official decision making in the service of national sovereignty is virtually a thing of the past . George Orwell's all-seeing eyes of "Big Brother" never was the monopoly of Communist Russia. Finally, the science of chemistry and genetic manipulation of human and plant genes have created the two terrible global diseases of AIDS and drug addiction (cocaine and crack, etc.) for destroying the military battalions of the human body, "the immune system." Television images attack the mind while cocaine and AIDS attack the body's military units—each one of them using the power of the pleasure principle.

It is a bizarre paradox that Boutrous Ghali, a man who crawled out from under the dense undergrowth and cobwebs of underdevelopment; a man not in his youth but in his seventies; a man chiseled from the timeless genius of the ancient Egyptian Pyramids, should be the one called upon to be the "inspiration" to transcending madness in a people. How does one "inspire" terror in the self-congratulating selfishness and greed of capitalism, now code-named "pro-democracy"? In the first week of May 1993, the British electorate disgraced the ruling Conservative Party and their "anti-people" policies, and yet the grandmother of those policies, Dame Margaret Thatcher, and others, are busy financing over two hundred "pro-democracy" propaganda organizations inside Russia and the rest of the former Soviet Union even in the face of a new and desperate poverty now hitting the peoples of those lands because of the ongoing dismantling of former Socialist economies. Can Boutrous Ghali be allowed by the governments that elected him (the permanent members of the Security Council) to reach out and "inspire" the voting peoples of Britain, or of bloodied former Soviet Union?

"We live in a period when governments, the basic units of the UN System, have less and less control over the forces that are shaping the future." The Mafia are non-governmental and trade in drugs globally. Tiny Rowland of LOHNRO (a multinational corporation) has pressured the Sudanese government and the SPLA groups back to the negotiating tables in Abuja and Nairobi. The AIDS disease is rumoured to have (and easily could have) been invented by biotechnology scientists working for multinational corporations. The present Pope in Rome and the Ayotollah Khomeni ran neck-to-neck in giving their respective religions new claws in international relations and cultures. The bomb-blasts planted by the "Shining Path" revolutionaries in Peru; by the ANC military wing in Johannesburg, and by the Irish nationalists (the IRA) in London's financial complex, became instant ingredients of world popular consciousness via satellite communications. Were they too entitled to ask Boutrous Boutrous Ghali to be an inspiration? Or perhaps to only some of them?

Boutrous Ghali's secretary generalship saw the UN playing world elections policeman for the defense of democracy in Angola, Western Sahara, and Eritrea. It organized one in Cambodia and was actively involved in elections in Mozambique, Somalia, and South Africa.

The rationale was to ensure that such elections were free and fair: no use of threats of loss of jobs and life by the contestants to coerce voters; no riggings, no kidnapping of and physical violence against other contestants, etc. The emphasis was on ensuring the expression of that power in the people to elect and throw out governments. No one ever thought of including the electing people of France, or in Britain or in the United States among those to be protected and aided by United Nations Observers or officials. This deviation does not deny the focus on empowering the people against organized powers. Maybe some time in the near future the use of television, manipulation of racist hatred, and fears of unemployment and poverty by governments in Britain, France, Germany, and the United States will be seen as factors that work against "free and fair elections." Until then, the UN will remain globally selective in its targets. Interestingly, President Clinton started his second term with a call for campaign funding reform in American politics.

This emphasis on empowering the people has many implications. For example, it raises the issue of mass poverty and impoverishment in the industrialized North and under-industrialized South by policies of governments which are among the permanent members of the Security Council. Poverty is also a loss of power. Mass poverty is loss of power by the people. It was a bell that tolled for the ears of the UN Secretary Generalship of Boutrous Ghali. Another example is that discrimination from access to resources (such as capital, respect, being listened to in public debate, recruitment into jobs, friendship, love, etc.) is a denial of an element of self-empowerment. Women and children, the so-called "indigenous peoples" (in Australia, Egypt, the United States, Brazil, Japan, Peru, etc.), the Indian, Colored and Black peoples in apartheid South Africa, are denied mass quantities of empowerment. Is it not time for a UN Secretary General to animate a Global Peoples Development Fund contributed to in perpetuity by the peoples of the world acting each individually for overcoming poverty and all other modes of disempowerment?

It can be argued that various organs of the United Nations are engaged precisely in this enterprise. The World Health Organization (WHO) fights malnutrition and disease as enemies of self-empowerment. The Food and Agricultural Organization (FAO), UNESCO, UNDP, UNIDO, etc., each fight on separate fronts of giving power to the people. But these were all Cold War institutions. They either sprang up to save the masses in war-devastated Europe from heeding the calls to revolution by communist parties in Britain, France, Italy, etc., or to lure away those parts of the world devastated by colonialism from becoming allies of the Soviet Union. Some did the jobs of penetrating local economies to prevent autonomous growth. This explains why the United States insisted on having the monopoly of the heads of UN agencies like UNICEF, UNDP, and the World Bank. UNDP is reported to "be spending $1.2 billion annually on projects in developing countries." That sum of money for generating development is less than the cost of manufacturing one of the wonder weapons which were used against Iraq in the Gulf War. Was Boutrous Ghali allowed to have such "deep commitment to the eradication of poverty," or be such an "independent and imaginative UN Secretary General" as to openly question the irrelevance and harmfulness of Cold War UN weapons in a time of giving power to the people and the promotion of democracy?

But, there are other dramatic frontiers too. After two terms of five years each, Boutrous Ghali would have been a very tired old man. Since all must pass, he would have needed wonderful memories "as hunting horns." One such tickling memory could have been the African, Chinese, Russian, Jewish, or African-American women whom he had groomed, and who eventually fought each other to a photo-finish for the job of the Secretary General of the post-Cold War—or rather, people-empowering—United Nations.

As it is, President Clinton probably decided that he had a date to keep with a private dream. He would invent the first Black African Secretary General of the United Nations. And his civil rights word said: let there be Kofi Anan?

Notes

1. Brian Urquhart and Eraskine Childers, *A World in Need of Leadership: Tomorrow's United Nations*. Uppsala: Dag Hammarskjold Foundation, 1990. The data here is from this work.